More Towels

More Towels

In Between the Notes

By Grant Jarrett

Writer's Showcase
San Jose New York Lincoln Shanghai

More Towels
In Between the Notes

Writer's Showcase
an imprint of iUniverse, Inc.

For information address:
iUniverse, Inc.
5220 S. 16th St., Suite 200
Lincoln, NE 68512
www.iuniverse.com

The people depicted in this book were all figments of my imagination.

Any resemblance to anyone, living or dead, is coincidental, and very unfortunate.

ISBN: 0-595-23798-3

Printed in the United States of America

"For Joanna, who seems to love me in spite of it all."

"Debauchery is perhaps an act of despair in the face of infinity."
— Edmond Louis Antoine de Goncourt

Contents

Prologue

B y the time I was born, in September of 1953 as I recall, it must have been clear that the Jarrett children were *all* destined to possess and eventually proudly display an exceptional musical facility. Keith was already considered a child prodigy (and a burgeoning pain in the ass), Eric, who would soon give up his instrument, the violin, was, at that point, following close behind, and Scott was most likely learning his piano scales with little effort. And although I don't doubt that we *did* share some common, probably genetic, musical aptitude, I believe the gift must have varied greatly among us in its intensity, and that the environment surrounding each of our still-unfolding stories—the volatile state of our family, the level of attention and support we were offered, our declining financial status, and all of the other indiscriminate variables that seem to direct and redirect the streams of our lives—greatly influenced our individual interest and enthusiasm.

Nevertheless, despite my own epic indifference, from 1969, when I was a mildly-talented, skinny, frightened twig of a sixteen-year old boy and Keith was developing an admirable reputation, until 1989, when I was a disillusioned, skinny, frightened, mendacious twig of a twenty-eight year old man (I had learned, by this time, to lie about my age) and Keith was famous for his enormous talent and his even larger ego, I made the great majority of my fluctuating, but always unimpressive income working as a "musician." I started early and I probably finished a little late. I played, with erratic proficiency, in top-forty bands, show bands, jazz trios, quartets, and big bands, in country bands, rock bands, and Irish bands. I worked with some of the best, and far too many of the worst, the famous and the infamous, the sublime and the appallingly absurd. And I slept with dozens of waitresses, singers, and dancers, wives and daughters of friends and strangers, pregnant teenagers, eager schoolgirls and young mothers, an extraordinary array of mostly sweet, lovely, though often deeply disturbed, young and not-so-young women. I was struggling with my raging hormones, my baser instincts, and my desperate desire to be loved. I was learning, often despite myself, to become an adult, and learning ever so slowly about life outside the theoretical safety of the nest.

Off and on throughout those twenty strange and obsessively licentious years, I considered—always with the understanding that I would never actually follow through (just having the idea was nearly as good and a hell of a lot less effort)—writing a book recounting that aimless, sometimes reckless, and often hilarious period of my life. I believed then that my experience was somehow unique. And it may have been, but because, unlike Shirley MacLaine (and my mother), for example, this is the only life I've had, I have nothing with which to compare it. So maybe I am wrong; maybe it was simply narcissism that drove me to finally put down on paper my most potent, most enduring recollections of those years that seemed, and still seem to me, such an odd and awkward mix of passion and indifference, desperation and desire, tears and laughter, timidity and aggression, fear and confidence, terrible ancient anger and tender childlike love. Whatever my motivation or inspiration might have been, once I began this journey backward, I was amazed how much detail I could, with a little effort, recall, and truly shocked at the range of emotions I apparently experienced in those years, as well as the enormous range of disparate behaviors I certainly demonstrated.

One of the many things I think I learned while writing this, ten years after the ugly fact, is that without the sometimes forgiving distortions of time and distance, it would probably not have worked; at least it would have been a very different book. And still, many questions remain unanswered. I don't know, I'll never know how "good" I might have been as a musician had circumstances been different. I'm not certain, in many cases, which of the choices I was faced with, were, or would have been the correct ones, and I don't know if I was as awful as

I've made myself appear or as lost as my recollections suggest. But who and what I am today is, to a substantial degree, the result of my years of playing and traveling and fucking and searching aimlessly, desperately for love, for music, for joy and laughter, and for a sense of purpose, searching most of all, I suppose, for some proof of my own worth and a reason to care.

Still, even after taking into consideration the wonderful curse of selective memory, the editing process, and a relatively limited focus, it seems odd and more than a little frightening to me that twenty years of my life, of anyone's life for that matter, could fit so comfortably into two-hundred-fifty odd (some odder than others) pages. But then (I keep telling myself) this was never intended to be the story of my life; it is merely a small part of the story of an aspect of my life from my limited, but hopefully interesting, perspective. These are the carefully pruned remains of my memories. Nevertheless, everything in my little book is as true as a reasonably sober forty-five-year-old's memory can be, though I have no doubt that my "truth" varies greatly from the truths of at least some of those with whom I shared the rocky ride, and particularly those unfortunate enough to find themselves described on these pages. My story, or this part of it, is not really about sex or love or music; it is the story of a sliver of a time in a life, the incomplete story of how I learned to be whatever it is that I have become.

My journey was a circuitous one, and looking back, it seems that my apparent survival, both emotionally and corporeally, is a consequence of life's arbitrary nature, and a testament to the robust human resilience that continues, even today, to astonish and impress me, when it's not scaring the shit out of me. A testament too, I suppose, to the powerful distraction afforded by ceaseless activity, and the aid and comfort that simple heartfelt psychotic laughter can bring.

1

Don't Worry That it's Not Good Enough for Anyone Else to Hear...

When I began playing music for a living I was very young, and not very good; fortunately, at that time and place, talent was not a critical requirement. Although I did appear to have some unrefined natural ability, what was far more important to prospective employers, was that I was tractable and reasonably presentable. And I was willing to work cheap. By the age of fifteen, I'd played at high school dances, love-ins, college fraternity parties, resort hotels, battles of the bands, and mostly in a great variety of garages in Northeastern Pennsylvania's Pocono Mountains. And in the winter of 1969, at the age of seventeen, I went on the road.

The first group with which I was unfortunate enough to travel was a self-contained show-band led by Fred Waring Jr., a recovering alcoholic, and the eldest son of the had-been bandleader and blender inventor whose limited celebrity dissolved in the nineteen-fifties almost as swiftly as it had materialized in the forties. Fred's third wife, Rochella, was the featured singer, and there was a mediocre comedy team consisting of two beyond middle-age weasels who tried hard (though never quite hard enough) to be another Dean Martin and Jerry Lewis, and got along just about as well. Alex Gergar played Hammond organ, Tom Perkins played electric bass, and my older brother, Scott, who sang backup in the shows and lead in the dance sets, played electric and acoustic guitars. The handsome bandleader, when he deigned to play at all, was a surprisingly proficient trombonist. And yes, there *is* such a thing.

We were probably no worse, and possibly a little better than some of the other bands on the same circuit. But actually, now that I think of it, maybe I'm wrong. Maybe we *were* worse. Yes, I think we were. In any case, we were a strange crew, ranging in age from seventeen to fifty-five and clad every night in matching burgundy three-piece velvet suits and ruffled white shirts. I believe we were billed as *The Fred Waring Junior Show, featuring the comedy team of Dick Chase and Bud Mitchell and Starring Rochella York.* This, though, was almost thirty years ago, so if I have misspelled a name or two, I almost sincerely apologize.

The first stop on the unwieldy ensemble's first and only road trip was The Hawaiian Cottage, a nightclub in Cherry Hill, New Jersey that was garishly adorned with imitation bamboo and lush plastic tropical fruits and flowers. A regular at the gaudy nightclub, and the act with whom we shared the stage in alternate sets, was an ostensibly Hawaiian, sword-swallowing fire-eater—a tall, broad-chested and very friendly fellow who taught me some card tricks that I still occasionally perform when I want to clear a room.

I don't recall much about our first week in Cherry Hill, but during the second week of our two-week engagement my mother came to hear us, bringing with her my pretty fifteen-year-old "Junior Miss" girlfriend, Jackie Bunninger. Jackie was (with the exception of an awkward one-night-stand in room 222 of the Minisink Hills Holiday Inn, where in a drunken frenzy I clumsily mauled the still-shod daughter of Dotty Dodgin, an unexceptional wreck of a pseudo-jazz drummer who had happily supplied us with the Cold Duck I guzzled and the pot her teenaged daughter smoked to get us in the "mood," and was, I assume, getting stoned with her ear to the floor in room 322, one floor above us) the first girl with whom I ever had sex. In spite of her father's apparent (and probably understandable) antipathy for me, Jackie had somehow arranged to stay overnight in New Jersey—an unexpected pleasure, for me, if for no one else. Thanks Mom.

Our engagement at The Hawaiian Cottage was intended as a paid rehearsal, an opportunity to fine-tune our fledgling act and expand our limited repertoire before moving on to some other dump. As it turned out, it was also the beginning of some ugly battles between Fred and Rochella, Dick and Bud, Dick and Bud and Fred and Rochella, and Rochella and the band, and on and on and on and on, and if the magnitude of the talent in that menagerie had approached five percent of the magnitude of the conceit, we would all be rich and famous and I would have had to change the names you've almost certainly never heard before and undoubtedly never will again. Unless they sue me.

Although Rochella was tall and fairly attractive, and was blessed with a pair of prominent high-slung breasts, she had about as much sex appeal, even to a horny teenager, as a mildewed scrubbing sponge, and she possessed a thin, piercing voice that, whether she was speaking or singing, was always just a few irksome degrees north of where it should have been—a voice that was sharp in every sense of the word. Because we understood why the well-assembled wife of the bandleader was there, *most* of us begrudgingly accepted her. Dick and Bud seemed to feel no compulsion to treat her particularly well, but the rest of us were constrained to endure our frustration and shame in relative silence.

At times, those first weeks, when it was just the quartet performing dance sets comprised of top-forty hits with a smattering of my brother's increasing repertoire of original material sneaked in, it was fun, and even exciting. We were learning, like paid apprentices, to be musicians and entertainers, and we were learning about another kind of life. The shows, on the other hand, were painful and embarrassing, in spite of the endless, tense rehearsals. Finally, after two weeks in New Jersey, we set out toward Winnipeg, Manitoba, Canada, North America, Earth, where we were booked in a newly opened nightclub, the name of which I have happily forgotten.

So...

While my brother and I plowed through the blinding blizzard that blanketed nearly half the nation, in his drafty, dilapidated, red Ford Falcon convertible, Alex and Tom, who had departed hours before us, were creeping along in Fred's sputtering two-tone Volkswagen van, overloaded with instruments and amplifiers. Fred and Rochella struggled through the icy mess at six gallons per mile and about as many miles per hour in their ponderous green and beige Winnebago. But the alleged comedians, who were being paid more than any of us for doing far less work just about as well, flew first-class—an early slap in the face of my still-innocent notions of justice.

Confident that we were making good time despite the inclement weather, Scott and I forged ahead, stopping only for bathrooms, food, and fuel until we arrived at the Canadian border, where the grim uniformed officers of the border patrol had already disassembled the Volkswagen Van and most of its contents in an enthusiastic but ultimately futile search for contraband fruits and vegetables. When they'd finally finished tearing our vehicles apart and interrogating us, it was so late that we missed our own opening night. I think they were just having a good time—impotent little men, feeling momentarily powerful. I hated them.

And so it was well after midnight when those of us who'd been apprehended at the border finally arrived at the club. What we soon learned was that Fred and Rochella were still in transit somewhere in the heart of the worsening storm. But Dick and Bud were waiting on an empty stage with the disgruntled club owner, Jimmy Ginakis, whose name I recall only because I referred to him, in his absence, of course, as Jimmy Gymnastics. We had already finished unloading our equipment, setting up the stage, and performing a sound-check when, late in the early morning, with the snow still spiraling down, Fred and his wife finally materialized, cold and weary, and just in time to apologize to Jimmy and get us all checked in to our rooms.

The downtown hotel where we were registered was clean and comfortable, and each of us had his own private room, which, as I would later learn, was an unusual luxury for traveling musicians. But there was one other notable peculiarity: there were strip shows on the small stage in the cafeteria-style restaurant three times a day. There was the lunch stripper, the dinner stripper, and the late night extravaganza, which consisted of both the lunch stripper *and* the dinner stripper. I had never before seen anything like this, and initially could not believe my good fortune. It was during my first lunchtime striptease, however, that I discovered that there was something less than erotic about watching a slightly plump though vaguely attractive youngish woman clumsily disrobing and changing her own 45s mid-strip, while I, sur-rounded by a gaggle of sweating, hungry lechers, dug sleepily into an overdone burger and greasy brown fries. The only exciting aspect of the situation was the knowledge, or at least the optimistic belief, that the strippers too were staying there in my hotel, perhaps on my very floor. Every night, as I paced down the hall toward my room, I would hope to run into one of them, though I doubt now that I would have known quite what to do or say if I had.

Nevertheless, although this was only the beginning of my life on the road, I was rapidly becoming an exceedingly lustful young man. And in addition to the unrealizable temptation of the in-house strippers, there were the beautiful, long-legged, short-skirted waitresses in the club, the tallest and most beautiful of whom I fucked repeatedly in my bed and in the shower—at least in my more implausible masturbatory fantasies. I had become sexually active only a couple years before, but now, with the barrage of stimulation surrounding me, my overzealous libido was frighteningly alert. The music, such as it was, was virtually irrelevant. And it deserved to be. Still, we somehow survived our four-week stay in Winnipeg, and were even invited to return at some unspecified time in the future. For some inexplicable reason, they liked us. Cretins.

The band's next stop, following a far less dramatic border crossing and a much calmer drive, was a sprawling compound in Burlington, Iowa called The Pizzaz-a-torium. I'm not making this up. The entire multi-level "entertainment complex" was owned and managed by the wealthy family who also owned the leading antenna manufacturing company in the U.S., Burlington's single largest employer. It occurs to me only now that they may not be doing so well now that cable and satellite dishes have taken over the civilized world. Oh well.

Burlington is situated in the lower right hand corner of the state, very close to the Illinois border and not terribly far from Missouri. It is, or was, I thought, a very typical Midwestern town. Most everyone owned a pickup truck or two, they all talked and moved a little more slowly than I was accustomed to, and all of the females over the age of fourteen had husbands or children, though seldom both. My time there is mostly a blur, with a few exceptions: I remember missing Jackie and calling her from my room almost every night, I remember learning how to appreciate alcohol, and I remember driving over the Illinois border to purchase beer late one night with some girls we'd somehow picked up in Burlington. I slept with the cute little fifteen year old I met that night, and in the morning I recognized what I had dimly suspected in my drunken stupor the night before: she was exceedingly pregnant. At least I could be relatively certain there was no husband to come gunning for me in his pickup truck.

After our adventure in Burlington, much of which has been permanently obscured by the indescribable discomfort I felt for so many reasons that morning in Iowa, we headed back to Pennsylvania to regroup and decide on the future, if any, of our group. And I was glad to be going home.

But…

Immediately upon our return to the Poconos, Fred supplied us—the rhythm section—with a list of songs to learn for the dance sets, one of which was *The Carpenters'* saccharine hit, *Sing a Song*. While our leader and his screeching wife relaxed or bickered on a some warm beach, the four of us rehearsed with impressive regularity. But though we tried, we simply couldn't bring ourselves to learn that one deplorable song. I guess we had some integrity, or maybe it was just the capacity for shame, which by that time had already been getting plenty of exercise. But when we expressed to Fred our aversion to that nause-ating melody, he continued to stubbornly insist, from his comfortable distance, that we learn it. Demoralized, my brother and I staged a bloodless coup. We went off on our own with Alex and Tom, leaving the overpaid deadwood behind.

The Jarrett Brothers' Band worked sporadically in and around the Poconos for several months and *The Fred Waring Junior Show* was just an embarrassing stain on our collective history. And we never had to play that moronic song, some of whose lyrics seemed, and still seem, so mockingly apt. And I quote: *"Don't worry that it's not good enough for anyone else to hear…just sing…"*

Ugh.

2

Love, Peace, and Soul

In the years following my brief stints with *The Fred Waring Jr. Show* and *The Jarrett Brothers' Band*, I earned some of my wages playing music in and around the Poconos. But to supplement that meager and inconstant income, I also worked, first as a delivery truck driver for Stroudsburg Candy Company, and then (having migrated with an appropriate sense of apprehension to New York City with my friend Brett) as a mailroom messenger at N.W. Ayer, the ad agency where Brett was already employed and where I would eventually become head of the reproduction department. One of the things I learned while in New York was that it is possible, though not particularly pleasurable, to survive on a diet consisting almost exclusively of spaghetti, peanut butter and jelly, corned beef hash and eggs, and, most often, an uninspired effluvial coagulation of fried potatoes and onions. But outside of some infrequent and unsatisfying work in the clubs and in the studio with *The Bob Lenox Trio*, a "jazz" group with which the ubiquitous Brett was the bass player, my musical career remained relatively stagnant, my stomach, unsettled.

I guess the most notable event in the otherwise unremarkable short-lived history of *The Bob Lenox Trio* was the Saturday night concert at Town Hall in Manhattan. We were booked that night as the warm-up band for *Captain Beefheart*, a peculiar "underground" group, similar in some vague way, I suppose, to Frank Zappa's *Mothers of Invention*. I remember waiting nervously backstage as the vast hall slowly filled, thinking to myself that this might well be the beginning of my inevitable rise to stardom. At eight o'clock, as I was planning the details of my increasingly promising future, someone gave us the signal to go out and begin our brief set. But buoyed by transitory visions of grandeur, I announced, "I'm not going out there 'til the hall is full and the audience is silent." And the idiots thought I was serious. They actually waited another fifteen minutes, until all the seats were taken, before sending us out to embarrass ourselves. Which, I'm now certain, we did.

Some time in 1973, after a little over a year in New York, I relocated again, this time to Bynner Street in Boston, where I shared a small two-bedroom apartment with my friend Mark, a fellow-drummer from Pennsylvania who had just enrolled to serve time at The Berklee School of Music. And it was in Boston—where my life as a traveling musician truly began—that I would encounter corroborating evidence that my dimpled stage smile was far more crucial to my success than was my competence as a drummer, and that my limited skills would pose no impediment whatsoever to my continued employment. But there was an even more astonishing discovery just ahead. I would soon learn, with a combination of disbelief and lustful delight, that even a skinny, funny looking, and very mediocre drummer could have his filthy way with a variety of comely young women. Or maybe what I really discovered was that a variety of comely young women were desperate or vulnerable enough to sleep with a skinny, funny looking, and very mediocre drummer. I was less concerned, however, with the lessons than with the results.

The first group with which I worked in Massachusetts was a show band called *Love, Peace, and Soul*. I *swear* I'm not making this up. One moderately talented black girl, Yma, also known as "Love" or "Soul"—I'm not sure which—stood between a short, cute white guy, Frank—probably "Love" but possibly "Peace"—and a tall, untalented, sweat-drenched mulatto, Mitch—either "Peace" or "Soul"—doing poorly choreographed steps almost in unison while singing a questionable selection of once popular songs in several dance sets and one or two really awful "theme" shows an evening. And it was another ugly contest of overgrown egos—egos that, by all rights, should not have been able to survive at all in earth's atmosphere. This, by the way, was another exceptionally well-dressed unit. Initially sporting snug black pants with matching vests or jackets (all tailored dozens of times to fit a series of disparately built "musicians") over one of an unsightly variety of puffy pastel shirts, we eventually graduated to a selection of equally appealing jump suits that may well have been fashioned from very old upholstery.

And yet...

One desperate night during my first two weeks with the band, I was surprised to find myself unenthusiastically fucking sweaty Mitch's girl-friend, an utterly unexceptional woman to whom I was not even faintly attracted. I think I just did it because I found him so terribly annoying, and because I realized I could. And a couple weeks later I fell in transi-tory lust with a slender and very pretty lass I met in the club in Framingham in which we were then performing. It took a lot of time and strained the narrow limits of my self-confidence—I was certain I would be rejected—but I eventually asked the soft-spoken, dark-haired waif to "*please* come home with me."

Because of my innate insecurity, I was astounded by this lovely stranger's willingness to accede to my unambiguously licentious entreaty. But not nearly as astounded as I was early the following morning when my phone rang and I crawled over Debby, or Donna or whatever the hell her name was and found myself talking with my girl-friend, Jackie.

So...

In a desperate effort to keep them both unaware of the precarious position I was in, I did my best to act as though I was casually chatting with an old buddy. But when, at the end of our strained, abbreviated conversation, Jackie said, "I love you," my heart jumped and I immedi-ately began to breed perspiration. When I finally caught my breath, I muttered something like, "Well great, then we'll talk soon." Unsatis-fied, she repeated herself. The temperature in the shrinking room dou-bled and again I made a clumsy attempt at an escape. But she wasn't going to let me off the hook. Finally she asked, with an audible pout, "Aren't you going to tell me you love me?" I was trapped; there was nowhere to hide. And so I glanced over at the lovely figure sprawling naked on the sheets next to me, and, as the sweat poured off my brow like a steaming cataract of doom, I mumbled, "I love you too," before hanging up the phone.

To her credit, and my relief, my new friend said, "I guess that was your girlfriend."

"Yes, it was," I responded, blushing brightly, filling the dark room with an eerie, blood red light.

She looked over at me and smiled, "It's alright. I have a boyfriend too."

My sentence was commuted. We got up and fried eggs on my forehead.

3

The Streets of San Francisco

For months I suffered with this dreadful assemblage, traveling from Concord, New Hampshire to Jacksonville, Florida and north again to Rhode Island. In Concord I met Ann Croteau, an appealing young woman whom I dated for a few weeks before glancing down at her one morning and noticing that, in that particular light, with those particular shadows, and from just the right (or wrong) angle, she bore a frightening resemblance to Karl Malden. I would never ask her out again. And it was sad. She was a sweet, good-looking girl who got caught for just a moment in a mischievous play of light and shadow that would most likely never be repeated. But I was unwilling to take that terrible gamble. I knew I could never look at her again without thinking of *On the Waterfront* or *The Streets of San Francisco*.

In Jacksonville, where I learned of our shy but incredibly capable bass player, Bob Colby's heroin addiction (he had the stuff mailed to him from Boston every week), I had no success at all. There were a couple of close calls, but the only night I spent with a female there was the night that a soft-spoken young unfortunate who had fallen hopelessly in love with Frank ("Love" or "Peace") ingested an overdose of pills after discovering that she was just one of three or four other young unfortunates he was poking between shows. When I learned of her unsavory snack, I rushed her to the nearest emergency room, where they pumped her stomach while I stood by, worrying about her survival and wondering if she would be in the mood for romance if and when she recovered, and, if so, what her breath would be like.

And in Rhode Island, the last place *Love, Peace, and Soul* would have the poor taste to work, and where, for some reason, I was amazingly popular, I found myself happily, but very discreetly juggling several sex-or love-crazed local girls. Life was complicated, but pretty good, and I was learning to smile a sincere if somewhat diabolical smile both onstage and off.

Love, Peace, and Soul was the second band (though certainly not the last) with which I worked, wherein the alleged "stars" were clearly the least essential, the least gifted components. So when we realized that we could, the rest of us rid ourselves of the two guys up front and became a smaller, better, and more efficient band, a band in which each member would earn more money than he or she had in the prior arrangement. The only problem was that I would have to learn to sing.

And…

When the remaining band members agreed to take a week off before getting back to work in our new, more-compact configuration, I decided to pay an unannounced visit to my mother and grandmother back in Pennsylvania.

I borrowed a car and drove home quickly, growing increasingly eager to see my family and friends as I neared the familiar countryside, but when I arrived at the modest little house my mother was then rent-ing in the woods along Broadhead's creek, there was no one there. Because my grandmother very rarely left the house, it didn't take long for me to become concerned. So I made a few phone calls, and within a couple anxious hours, my friend Bert, having heard from his parents of my distress, phoned to tell me that, though he didn't know any details, he thought he'd heard something about my grandmother being taken to the hospital. I called the local hospital to confirm the discouraging news and dashed out to see her.

Even now, as I write this, I can remember Anna's crooked mouth, and the look of fear and frustration on her drawn and sallow features as she tried to speak, gazing helplessly up at me from a narrow bed in the tiny rectangular room she shared with some other unfortunate stranger whose face I never saw. I remember wiping her chin, gripping her cold, contorted hand—a hand that I can still see and feel if I close my eyes—and telling her how much I loved her. She seemed to be trying to smile, but half of her sinking, almost colorless face refused to comply, and soon, despite my efforts, I began to cry. I'd wanted to allay her fears and make her feel safe, but I just stood there holding her gnarled hand in mine and sobbing. When I left the hospital that day, I knew I'd let her down; I didn't have the strength to conceal my own emotions. It was too much of a shock. My sweet, dear grandmother had lived with our family since long before I was born, and, though I was certain she was slipping away, I simply couldn't conceive of losing her.

In the dull, depressing days following my arrival in Pennsylvania, my grandmother gradually, partially improved, and soon, still weak and crippled from the stroke, she was able to return home. But of course she would never fully recover.

4

Fire, Theft, and Fresh Green Beans

I t was about nine o'clock in the evening when I arrived back in Boston, where several fire trucks obstructed the hazy entrance to Bynner Street. When the trucks' proximity to my apartment building registered in my weary brain I grabbed the first parking space I could find and sprinted toward the building. There was still thick black smoke pouring from the building's main entrance, which was about two feet to the right of the separate entrance to the apartment where Mark and I lived, but the firemen were already strolling out, carrying axes and retracting a flaccid hose. As I stumbled blindly through the dark, fuliginous mist that remained, I asked one of them what had happened.

"This guy over here was cooking a pork chop or something, and I guess he fell asleep. It got a little out of hand; his whole damned kitchen was incinerated." And there in the hallway, outside his open door, unshaven in a shabby plaid bathrobe, stood our neighbor, covered with soot and wobbling with sleepy intemperance. I gazed at him with silent disgust. As I walked toward my own door he mumbled with an intoxicated slur, "Well I never complain about your *music*." With the exception of a permanent ashy odor, our apartment was unscathed.

After playing around the Boston area for several weeks, the first stop for the newly formed band, *Fat City Brass*—a band which, despite our ill-chosen name, had only two horn players—was a small club in Dover, Delaware, where, instead of the usual matching hotel rooms, we were put up in a house, and where we all got along fairly well, learning new material while getting to know and mostly like one another better. The two things I recall most clearly about our otherwise uneventful three-week stay in Delaware, are the large man in the plain white tee shirt who sat near the stage almost every night, chewing noisily on his crumbling beer glasses, and the night we were robbed. Actually, the house we were staying in was burglarized while we were at work. It was probably the club owner's way of offsetting his losses.

I think it was a Friday or Saturday night when we returned to the house and found the door broken and our property spread chaotically around the floors. Jamie lost an expensive guitar, a good 35mm camera, and a couple hundred dollars in cash, and the others lost cheap cameras and smaller quantities of money. I'd been saving for several months to buy a car, and storing the gradually growing wad of bills in an envelope in the side pocket of my dilapidated old suitcase. So when it finally dawned on me what had occurred, I rushed into the room I shared with Cliff. My flimsy suitcase was upside down on the floor, and its contents, mostly threadbare socks and faded underwear, strewn about the room. But the envelope was resting on the floor next to the bed, still thick with tattered tens and twenties. I was lucky. But I believe I was also, at least for an uncomfortable minute, a suspect; after all, I was the only one who hadn't actually lost anything. And Jamie, who was born and raised in Delaware, was duly enraged. At three o'clock in the morning, he charged outside and repeatedly screamed to a sleeping Dover, "I hate Delaware," and, "Fuuuuuuck."

A week later, still in Dover, I exchanged six-hundred dollars in cash for a red 1969 Datsun that looked as though it had been painted by a nervous man with a second-hand broom, but which would run just fine, in warm weather at least, for a surprisingly long time. That rickety little car afforded a type of freedom, or at least the illusion of freedom (and what difference is there?), that I'd desperately desired.

From Delaware we journeyed north again toward Boston, stopping at Cliff's parents' house in rural Connecticut for a homemade dinner.

It was at Cliff's childhood home that I tasted my first real green beans, and it is still a surprisingly potent memory.

I had never before eaten any vegetable that hadn't come from a box or a can, and that hadn't had the life and crunch boiled mercilessly out of it, and consequently I hated anything green. But these exquisite, crisp green beans, which had come, that very day, from a nearby garden, were absolutely amazing. This was my introduction to the wonderful world of fresh vegetables. My horizons were widening. Nevertheless, to this day I remain firm in my fervent and, I think, entirely reasonable antipathy toward Brussels sprouts and the lowly lima. *They* have no place in a civilized society, except, possibly, as instruments of torture. *They* are the "*punitive vegetables*"©.

Back in Boston we played at some of the local clubs while beginning our search for another female singer, not to replace Yma, but to "broaden" our appeal. And after several disappointing albeit hilarious auditions, we settled upon Cheryl Yorkavich, the former Miss Ohio, who, while not a powerful singer, was quite lovely to look at, and perfectly willing to relinquish the "avich" for the sake of brevity and marketing. The first booking for our newly expanded group was in beautiful Muncie, Indiana.

Since I had my own car now, and a little time to spare, I left Boston for Muncie two days early, stopping again in Pennsylvania to visit my mother and my gradually recovering grandmother, and to try to spend some time with the old friends I'd shunned on my previous trip. I'm not certain now that it was a part of my plan to get together with my ex-girlfriend, who had recently terminated our long relationship. Nonetheless, Jackie and I somehow ended up going out to dinner and then spending the night groping one another in my old bedroom. I had missed Jackie, and being with her again made me realize how much she still meant to me, but as I escorted her to her car in the too-early morning, she made it painfully clear that our night together had not been an emotionally meaningful experience for her. As she stood next to the boat-like burgundy Chevy Impala her parents had handed down to her as punishment for getting her driver's license, she said, "I just wanted to see if it would be the same." "Was it," I asked, confused and hurt. "Yes," she responded coldly. "Goodbye."

I suppose the things that remain in one's memory do so because of their significance or potency, and I still recall very clearly the gloomy emptiness I felt when I realized that my first love and I would most likely never be together again. Or maybe it was just the wound to my delicate ego that I felt that brisk morning in Pennsylvania. Somehow, the latter seems more likely.

5

What's Your Signs?

Dreary and bland, Muncie was not an outwardly appealing city, but it was work, and at this point in my life it was a much-needed distraction. And once again the band was housed in a comfortably furnished home, rather the more traditional hotel rooms. And once again Cliff and I shared a room.

It was on our opening night at the bustling Muncie nightclub where we were engaged, that I noticed an absolutely lovely waitress. Night after night, set after set, I ogled her, making awkward attempts to pass close to her whenever the opportunity arose, or could somehow be forced. I ordered beers I didn't want and trudged the long way around the dance floor just to be able to see her adorable face again. Finally, after endless silent rehearsals, I timidly approached her.

"Hi" I said, averting my eyes like a schoolboy, "Can I ask you a question?" I glanced back up.

"Sure." She smiled a sweet and truly unforgettable smile.

"Are you married?" I asked, and my heart shot up into my tight, dry throat.

"Yes." Her tone seemed almost apologetic. "I am."

"That's very disappointing," I said. "Well, I think you're beautiful anyway and if you weren't married I would want desperately to ask you out."

"Well that's awfully nice."

"I really hope I haven't made you uncomfortable," I said, and peered around us to be certain we weren't being heard.

"Not at all," she said. "I think you're very sweet."

I was saddened and disappointed, and yet she *did* appear to like me at least enough to be gentle with me in a potentially humiliating situation. That in itself seemed something of a victory, and after my visit to Pennsylvania, my damaged ego was in desperate need of a victory—any victory. So although I knew nothing would come of it, I continued flirting with Carolyn, chatting with her whenever I was offered the opportunity. I simply could not help it. And she continued to act as though she liked me, at least a little.

But...

Two or three nights after that first encounter, I noticed that Carolyn seemed distracted and a little unhappy. When I asked her what was wrong, she moved closer to me and told me in a near whisper that her husband, Steve, had planned to go away for the weekend, but had, at the very last minute, changed his mind. She was disappointed, she explained, because she'd bought a bottle of wine in hopes that she and I could take advantage of his absence and spend some time together. My heart raced and my penis perked up like a puppy waiting for a biscuit. I could not believe my good fortune, or, for that matter, my bad luck. When she suggested that we might still go out for a snack after work that night, I (always a selfless slave to the needs and desires of others) reluctantly acceded.

Later that endless and magical night, as I reached over to help her with her seatbelt, Carolyn grinned at me and said, "I'm not really hungry, are you?" I leaned toward her, engaged her seatbelt, and kissed her softly on the lips. Strangely, the hunger that had been building in my stomach abated, or relocated.

Although it was already getting late, there were several cars parked in front of the house where the band was staying when we pulled up, one of which Carolyn thought she recognized. So while she sat waiting in my car, I went inside to see what was going on and to ask Cliff if he could find something to do for the next month or so. Cliff and Jamie were entertaining a few guests in our living room, and they seemed to be enjoying themselves, so I waited for a minute before pulling Cliff aside to make my furtive supplication. Without a moment's hesitation, Cliff said he would be happy to comply. He was a good and understanding friend, and at that moment I felt a fondness for him that I've seldom felt for another man. The only difficulty remaining was getting Carolyn past the throng unnoticed.

Just minutes later, I found myself eagerly pulling an adorable, giggling woman through my bedroom window, and within a short time Jackie Bunninger was a vague, distant memory, swiftly fading, along with much of the rest of my childhood and most of the phone numbers I'd memorized. And I still recall my first, or maybe it was my second impulse, as I gazed up at this unreal image of warm, naked perfection: I wanted to turn the page for another view. That night was the strange and wonderful beginning of what would be one of the most significant relationships in my life.

Carolyn got home to her husband very late that night, but in the morning when I awoke, uncharacteristically energetic and madly, insanely in love, she was waiting outside for me, with an ice cream cone and a long, tender kiss. After that it was simply a question of where and when we could spend time together without getting caught, and how much passion we could expend without damaging the ozone layer or triggering an earthquake.

When her cousin complicated our dissolute plans by visiting on our mutual night off, we deliberately and very rapidly got her so drunk on redundant pitchers of beer at Pizza Hut that she lay unconscious (or dead for all we knew or cared at that moment) in the cramped backseat of my car, while Carolyn and I sneaked into the house and made love. It wasn't until several joyful hours and orgasms later that the car horn finally began to blare.

And when Carolyn's parents came for the weekend to spend time with their daughter and her husband, she invited me over, introducing me to them as her new "friend" from the band. Carolyn and I flirted without regard to the risk, making references that, hopefully, only we would understand, while the five of us sat around clumsily chatting about nothing. It was exhilarating, and I guess it was kind of nasty, but at the time it really didn't seem so terrible. We were in love, and, of course, that was all that mattered.

At the club we passed notes like schoolchildren, and we stole passionate kisses whenever and wherever we could, and as far as we knew no one suspected. We saw each other every day and nearly every night, and we made love at every opportunity.

In time, Carolyn taught me to prepare and insert her diaphragm so we could avoid that inevitable awkward and unromantic interruption on those few occasions when she hadn't anticipated the need or the opportunity. I learned to squeeze a circle of thick, white contraceptive jelly around the circumference, smear a small dollop around the center with my finger, fold it carefully in half, and slide it gently inside her while she lay smiling up at me, eagerly awaiting the next slow insertion. I've never fully understood why I found this so particularly touching, but I did nonetheless, and I guess I still do. And I shared with her my love of nature, and taught her that some men actually enjoy performing oral sex, and care very much about pleasing the women they love.

I'm certain the rest of the band was out meeting people and having great frolicking fun in Muncie while all of this was going on, but I was unconcerned with almost anything outside of my wonderful, impossible obsession with Carolyn. In time though, with the gentle prompting of my peers, I began to feel a little guilty about my seemingly antisocial behavior. And finally, on a lonely night when Carolyn couldn't find a way to get away from Steve (and God, was I jealous), I attended a party with my colleagues.

Jamie had never had great success with women, and was, understandably, not especially pleased about it. But at this particular gathering, he became involved in an extended intimate dialogue with an odd, though not unattractive, young woman. They spent much of the evening sitting on the couch, discussing astrology and other mystical myths he was willing to believe in, at least for the moment, if it would help his single-minded cause. And she seemed truly, if not exclusively, interested in him. Throughout most of the night Cliff and I kept a reasonable distance from the two, both out of respect for Jamie and because there was something a little odd about her. Eventually, and to silent approbation, Jamie left the party with the peculiar woman.

But...

Early the following morning, just as I was falling awake, a woman's voice came from what seemed like the general direction of Cliff's bed. I knew he'd gone to sleep alone, and so, my curiosity aroused, I remained immobile. I just listened quietly to this vaguely familiar voice, trying to make sense of an increasingly intriguing situation, with the blankets pulled up over my head.

"That's how us Virgos are," the voice confidently proclaimed.

"I didn't know that," Cliff mumbled, sounding just a little uncomfortable.

"Really? Well you know, Cliff, you remind me of my brother. I *love* my brother."

"Huh."

"I knew you were an Aries, I can always tell." It sounded like the woman from the party. "You know, I'm an Aquarius," she said proudly.

"I thought you just said you were a Virgo."

"Jamie is an Aquarius too, but, I don't know, he's kind of intense." My suspicions were confirmed; it was indeed Jamie's 'date.'

"Jamie's a...a great guy," Cliff said, sounding desperate, feigning enthusiasm.

"He's not like you, Cliff. You remind me of my father; he's a Cancer, like me."

"Uh...didn't you just say you were an Aquarius?"

She laughed. "It's really complicated, you know, but just I wanted to...you know, come in and see you," she said, laughing harder.

"Where *is* Jamie?" Cliff asked.

"He's out there all pissed off, just like my father." She suddenly began to cry.

I could contain my laughter no longer, and when it came it was like the explosion of an over-inflated balloon, blowing the covers off of my head. Triggered by my unexpected outburst, Cliff too lost control, and the two of us shook with waves of violent laughter while she just sat on the edge of his bed sobbing noisily. When Cliff and I finally regained our composure and dried our eyes, I tried to offer an apology, but just as I started to speak, *she* began laughing hysterically. A second later Cliff and I erupted yet again. When we all calmed down for a second time, I did apologize, explaining that I had been trying not to eavesdrop but that, under the circumstances, it had been extremely difficult. She told me that it was okay, and then added that I reminded her of her father. With Jamie crashing and thumping violently out in the kitchen, the confused, uneasy laughter began once more.

But suddenly she became silent; she seemed to be trying to figure something out. A minute passed before she looked over at me and announced, "There is something I want to ask you guys, but I'm just not sure you're ready to hear it."

"Let me guess," I said. "You want to sleep with both of us."

Cliff turned a lovely shade of crimson when she answered, "Yes."

I thought for a moment and said, rubbing my eyes, "I have something to say too, but I'm a little embarrassed and I don't really know you very well."

"You can say anything to me. I'm a Virgo."

I glanced over at Cliff. "Should I tell her?"

He, of course, had no clue what I was going to say, but played along skillfully. "Go ahead, Grant. I think she'll understand, she's a Virgo…etcetera."

"Well," I said, gazing grimly down at the floor, "I was in the army several years ago, and I was injured pretty badly." I looked up at her. "Jeez. It's awfully embarrassing, but…my penis was shot off in Vietnam."

"Wow, that is *so* sad." She began to sob as though her entire family had just died.

"Not really. It wasn't much of a penis." And the roaring, gut-wrenching laughter began anew.

Little more was said before Jamie, his red eyes blazing behind thick lenses, came hunting for her.

But…

That night when we got to the club, the police were leaving, dragging with them with the lunatic astrological nymphomaniac from hell. She had apparently run up on the stage while dinner was being served, and started screaming about her father and tearing off her clothes. She had probably requested the handcuffs. And Jamie contracted gonorrhea.

When the band's engagement in Muncie came to an end, it was very difficult for me to leave Carolyn behind. Still, despite our compelling desire to be together, it was sadly clear to both of us that there was, at this point, no way for her to come with me. After all, she had a job.

And so we agreed that we would have to somehow find a way to make it work, but reluctantly decided, in spite of the powerful temptation to run off together and live off fumes, not to be impulsive about it. I drove alone toward New Jersey, eagerly planning Carolyn's divorce and our ineluctable happy future together, sad, anxious, happy, and utterly terrified.

6

A Popular Guy

It was in Muncie that I learned a critical undeniable truth: when a man is entrenched in a passionate and gratifying relationship with a woman, he immediately, automatically becomes much more attractive and desirable to every other woman in the solar system. Though I did not act on them, my opportunities in this small Midwestern city seemed virtually limitless, and, to my astonishment, the magic followed me to New Jersey, where I would encounter the fetching and perfectly-proportioned Barbara Gluck.

Barbara played guitar and sang folk songs at dinnertime and throughout the evening on our band's nights off at The Wobbly Barn. She was surprisingly talented, and she was also, surprisingly, unashamedly interested in me. I spent quite a few evenings drinking shots of Jack Daniel's with her—it was Barbara who first introduced me to the quietly charming Mr. Daniel's. And though it wasn't always easy, I was able to keep a nearly appropriate distance. And Barbara was quite persuasive, subtly tempting me with her exceptional body while reminding me with amazing regularity that, after all, Carolyn was still sleeping with her husband every night. Nevertheless, I was able to restrain myself, though I did assure her that I would be more than willing to get to know her better if things didn't work out with Carolyn. As always, I was keeping the door open, preparing for an uncertain future, storing nuts for winter. Fortunately, Carolyn took a flight to Tom's River the following week.

All of this female attention was both wonderful and confusing. I did not believe I was attractive or interesting or talented or particularly bright. I thought that, at best, I might, on rare occasion, be vaguely cute, or mildly charming. And yet here I was, in love with a gorgeous married woman who was eager to walk out on her husband to spend time with me, while simultaneously being aggressively pursued by at least one other lovely and fascinating woman. And by the time I left New Jersey a third woman would express romantic interest in me. I was not improving a hell of a lot as a musician, but I was smiling broadly most of the time, and, for the moment at least, I was very much in love.

On our way toward Boston, Carolyn and I took at brief detour, stopping in Pennsylvania for a couple days. I still recall proudly introducing her to my mother, and then to some of my friends. I remember how sweet she was to my still-recovering grandmother, and I remember lying on a grassy ledge at the top of a cliff, making love with her in the afternoon to the muffled roar of a distant waterfall. As we were dressing that day, gazing down at the rushing stream that wound through the lush green valley below, a fawn approached us, coming nearly close enough to touch, sniffing at us before casually proceeding on its way. It seemed like nature's stamp of approval.

Carolyn stayed with me in Boston for more than a week, occasionally phoning Steve and telling him one partial lie or another. And although I continued to commute to and from a forgettable club in the upper right hand corner of Massachusetts, we had a wonderful time together. Our relationship was young and passionate, and we were still getting to know each other, teaching and learning from each other and growing even closer. And we never relinquished our childlike playfulness.

For example…

Late one night, toward the end of Carolyn's visit, Cheryl and the two horn players were crowded into the narrow backseat of my Datsun as we began the long drive back from the club. When Carolyn complained that she was tired and asked if she could lean over and rest her head on my lap, I had a pretty good idea what she was threatening. But

I didn't believe she would actually follow through with the backseat filled with our friends. I was wonderfully mistaken. It was a memorable if treacherous drive, and I wasn't nearly as talkative as usual. Nor was she.

We both knew, of course, that Carolyn would eventually have to go home again; there was a lot of unfinished business to attend to (parents, husband, etc.) if we were going begin to build our new life together. We were mature enough to realize (or dishonest enough to tell each other) that it wouldn't be fast or easy, but we were certain what we had was worth waiting, and, if necessary, fighting for. So with tears blurring my vision I put her on a plane back to Muncie. We would save our money and devise a plan. Somehow, we repeatedly assured each other, in action and in word, it would all work out.

Carolyn and I wrote to each other and spoke on the telephone nearly every day (my phone bill that first lonely month was over three hundred dollars, which, translated to today's currency, would be about two-hundred-fifty-thousand dollars). We discussed our future, and, despite some justifiable concerns, I began to enthusiastically plan my next visit to Muncie. Soon, to my astonishment, Carolyn informed her husband that she was in love with me, and that she wanted a divorce. And though Steve tried hard to convince her to listen to "reason," explaining that living with a musician was not going to be easy, that life with *him* would be safer and more secure, and though Carolyn must have realized that he was probably right, it didn't matter; she knew what she wanted—or thought she did. Or wanted to think she thought she did.

The band continued to work throughout New England, and I spent much of my free time worrying about how I was going to support two people on my modest and unreliable salary, and, for the first time, seriously contemplating other as yet undetermined employment options. And Barbara Gluck wrote frequently to ask how things were going with Carolyn and let me know she was still thinking of me. Barbara was sweet and quite patient, but I was not interested enough in bedding her to jeopardize my relationship with Carolyn. I was still expending virtually all of my time and energy searching for a way to secure a future with the woman I truly loved.

Finally, after six long weeks away from Carolyn, the band booked a three-week engagement in Burlington, Vermont, after which, we all agreed, we would take two weeks off. Carolyn ordered Steve to move out, and I booked a flight to Indiana.

7

Vermont Home Cookin'

I t was horrifically hot in Burlington—hotter, according to the sweat-drenched local residents, than it had ever been before—and the club where we performed, which was like a giant gymnasium with a bar, had no air-conditioning. Our housing, composed of four drab, steaming cabins a few miles north of town, was also lacking in that particular creature comfort, as was my car. I don't believe I have ever perspired so much. The heat at work and at "home" became so oppressive that more than once, after we'd finished playing for the night, two or more of us would stop at one of the "authentic" hotels along the route back to our musty cabins and creep into the unlit swimming pool for an illicit, but bracing, late-night dip.

Unfortunately, my friend and roommate, Cliff, had retired from the band, so I had to break in a new roommate, and the band had to break in a new bass player, which meant rehearsing yet again the music of which we'd long ago grown weary.

We spent the majority of our oppressive afternoons sitting lazily in the shade of the trees surrounding our cabins, praying for a rare cooling breeze while we talked through our repertoire with Steve. And only occasionally did one or another of us attempt a brief brave expedition into the blaring heat of the sun in an effort to sustain our deep New Jersey tans.

Inhabiting several of the other eight or so small cabins in the compound were tourists, transients, and a few locals—people, I suppose, who could not afford, or, for other reasons, chose not to secure more traditional lodging. And in one of the cabins on the opposite side of the broad sun-bleached lawn, there lived a darling little girl and her plain but pretty mother, long, straight straw-colored hair framing a constant sad smile. Between and sometimes during our outdoor rehearsals, I spent a lot of time playing with the child, and I eventually befriended her mother, whom I soon learned was unhappily involved in a precarious and abusive relationship with the likely father of her child.

One afternoon, as I was reclining alone on a rickety plastic lawn chair, the little girl skipped across the lawn and politely announced, "My mother wants to know if you want to have dinner with us tonight." "Sure," I responded, though I was not sure at all.

That evening the three of us sat around the table eating the dinner that, despite her evident poverty, this shy, sad woman had prepared. During the meal and through dessert we talked and laughed like a young happy family, and after we finished she put her adorable if gently resistant daughter to bed. When the little girl was finally silent, the two of us relaxed at opposite ends of her small couch, where we sipped cheap white wine by cheap candlelight and tried not to appear as uncomfortable as we both undoubtedly felt. But after about an hour of small talk and twitching, we both heard the rumble of a pick-up truck coasting down the gravel road that circumnavigated the courtyard. She jumped up, rushed to the window, and slid the corner of the curtain back to see if it was he. Fortunately it was not. Nevertheless, she was shaking and pale when she sat back down.

I took my time finishing the sugary wine, and after thanking her again for dinner, I gave her an innocuous but gentle kiss. I reminded her that I would still be there for another week, and wished her a good night before making my way across the dark lawn to my own gloomy oven. Of course I had no intention of visiting them again. I had no desire to hurt this unhappy soul's feelings, but I was in love with Carolyn, and there would have been no point in pursuing this, whatever it was or might have been, any further. Still, I haven't forgotten her or her adorable little daughter, and I don't think I'll ever forget the fear I saw on her pretty, anemic face when she heard that truck, or the sadness, when I left. I hope that they are okay, though it seems so terribly unlikely.

But...

During our final sweltering week in Vermont I became increasingly restless, and, for no apparent reason, concerned about my relationship with Carolyn. So in an attempt, I suppose, to divert my thoughts, I began to socialize with the small but faithful audience we had somehow cultivated. On the last Friday night of our stay, Steve and I befriended a couple of women who had become ardent fans. Steve was attracted to one of them, and I was happy to offer assistance to my new friend, and relieved to have the distraction. On every break we ambled back to their table, where we sat telling jokes, guzzling beer, and flirting. And it was a pleasant undertaking. The other woman was not at all unappealing. And what harm could possibly result from a little innocent flirtation?

After our final set of the evening Steve's new friend suggested a drive to Lake Champlain. Steve consented for both of us before taking me aside to persuade me to come along. "Otherwise," he entreated, with the pungent scent of carnal desperation on his breath, "it could become a little awkward."

So we drove our two cars to a small shore along the coast of the lake, where the four of us sat on the warm beach, drinking beer and enjoying the gentler night air. And when it became apparent that Steve and his friend wanted to be alone, as was the unspoken plan, I offered to escort the other woman home. Steve thanked me discreetly as we pulled away.

While we navigated the dark, narrow roads back toward town, the young woman and I talked some more. She described a miserable childhood, and complained that her life had never become what she had hoped, that she feared now that it never would. I put my hand on hers to comfort her. When we pulled in to the lot behind her apartment building she asked me if I felt like coming inside. With some reluctance, I apologetically declined. But as I leaned over to kiss her cheek, she cradled my face in her hands, planted her open lips on mine, and slid her hand to my crotch, pressing hard. I automatically returned her kiss, and she unbuttoned her blouse and drew my hand toward her exposed breast. With both hands she grasped my belt buckle and opened it before unbuttoning my jeans and tugging the zipper down. Then, leaning over me, she pushed her head toward my lap and slid my pants down around my knees. Sitting upright, I rubbed her back with one hand and reached around to her full breasts with the other as she greedily licked and sucked until I came.

As soon as she was sitting upright, she began to sob. But she would not speak and she mutely rebuffed my clumsy efforts to comfort her. She just said goodnight and thanked me before kissing me on the cheek and stepping out of the car. I would never see her again.

I'm still not certain why, aside from my innate concupiscence—the easiest, most obvious (though most difficult to pronounce) explanation—I allowed this to happen. What I *am* sure of is that I found ways afterwards to justify my behavior to myself and to the few others with whom I shared the story. Maybe Carolyn had been a little distant or noncommittal in a recent phone conversation—she *had* made several references to a waiter she'd befriended at the new restaurant where she was working. Maybe I blamed the alcohol, the woman's aggressiveness, or the sultry night air. But wherever I attempted to lay the responsibility for my debauchery, it didn't help much. I was guilty and ashamed, and maybe a little frightened about what this might suggest about my character. The fact is that I was probably fully aware from the beginning of that night, from the first time I sat at their table and received a friendly smile in return for the one I'd proffered, that there was potential for something like this to occur. I didn't have ignorance as an excuse, at least for this. I had always tried hard to view myself as a warm, decent person, but the more I learned about who I really was, and what I was capable of, the more difficult it seemed to become. Of course that didn't stop me from behaving as I did.

8

Timing is Everything

I was expected in Muncie the following Monday evening, and in anticipation of my visit, Steve had grudgingly moved out of the apartment he and Carolyn had shared throughout their marriage. But my departure from Boston was delayed for a day. When Carolyn, looking as enticing as I'd remembered, picked me up at the Indianapolis airport on Tuesday afternoon, she revealed that on the previous night an unfamiliar man who apparently bore some vague resemblance to me, at least in terms of height and hair-color, had come in alone for dinner at the restaurant where she was now working. After dinner, he'd remained at the bar for a while, engaging her in polite conversation (and probably flirting) before paying his check and leaving. The ill-fated man was now in the hospital, recovering from the bloody beating that had taken place outside the restaurant, a beating that had evidently been intended for me. I suppose I should have sent him a card or flowers or something, but I did not. And perhaps I should have been afraid for my own safety, but for no reason I can now conceive, I was not. Perhaps I simply enjoyed the drama.

In spite of the violence that preceded my visit, violence that had been meant for me but had fallen on an unfortunate stranger with terrible timing, Carolyn and I had a wonderful time together that week. Nevertheless, that was also when the subtle haunting doubts about her fidelity began to surface. As I look back now, I believe Carolyn was in love with me, at least for a while. But I also believe that, perhaps for the first time, she was beginning to sense a freedom she'd never known before. This beautiful woman had been stifled for so long, and suddenly there were limitless possibilities. She may also have been wrestling with some of the same demons with which I'd been doing battle for most of my life. And why not?

In the hectic weeks following my second sad departure from Muncie I continued to cling to my love for Carolyn and my hopes for our future, but as time passed and the distance between us remained, I became increasingly concerned. Soon she started divorce proceedings, and shortly after that she rented an apartment with another single woman. But she was also making new friends. She was no longer always home when I called her late at night, and I was jealous and terribly afraid. She always had fairly reasonable, if not entirely credible explanations for her nocturnal absences, but I felt I was losing her, nonetheless. Although I had no way of being certain, and despite my own behavior, the fear and jealousy were driving me insane.

During the first week of our three-week booking in a small club in Hyannis, Massachusetts, my now obsessive suspicions about Carolyn's commitment to our relationship became nearly unbearable. And early in our second week at the club, Tom's younger brother was killed in an automobile accident in Minnesota. With our regrets and best wishes, Tom left for the funeral immediately. The rest of the band remained behind, compensating in every way we could for our saxophonist's tragic absence. Meanwhile, I was planning another visit to Muncie.

Nevertheless...

Dottie Jergenson, a waitress at the club in Hyannis, was tall and well formed, with substantial curves and long blond hair—not as delicately, gracefully beautiful as Carolyn, but lovely and completely unapproachable nonetheless. I tried, just for the distraction and the exercise, to flirt with her, but I was suddenly tongue-tied. I would attempt to look her in the eye or speak to her, but in spite of my prior triumphs I continually failed. It was becoming a frustrated and somewhat embarrassing obsession. Finally, on our last night at the club, I approached her—maybe just to prove to myself and my colleagues that I could—and blurted out the following sentence, "Hi I really think you are incredible and I'd love to go out with you here let me give you my phone number I won't ask for yours call me please if you feel like it goodbye." She said, "Okay." I said, "Huh?" With intimidating directness, she announced, "I'll call you."

The following week I went to Muncie to see Carolyn for what would be the last time. When she picked me up at the airport in Indianapolis, she looked different; her hair was shorter and she had gained a few pounds. And though she was still very affectionate, it was clear to me that something was not quite the same. We went out to dinner and drank wine together, and, back at her new apartment, we made love. We did exactly what we had always done, but I knew something was missing, or at least out of place. One evening when she was at work I found an open box of condoms in her drawer next to a half-empty tube of Gynol II, and although Carolyn had explanations for these things too, by that time I guess it didn't matter. Though I never really understood why, we both knew that it was over. In spite of my own dubious conduct, I was devastated by this loss, and though I would try hard, and in many ways, I would not fully recover for a very, very long time.

9

No, I've Never Been Fucking Mellow

The following week, back in Boston, I telephoned Barbara Gluck, and within days, true to her word, she came to visit. Barbara couldn't replace Carolyn of course, she couldn't make everything okay, and I think she realized all of that, but she was a sweet and sexy friend and a fervently willing diversion. She was understanding and caring, and she gently comforted me while fucking me like a rabid antelope.

Barbara stayed with me for about a week, and I only called her "Carolyn" once, at which time she was kind enough to act as though she hadn't heard the indefensible gaffe.

Two weeks later our band was booked again at The Wobbly Barn, where Barbara and I had first met, and where we continued to spend our time together inadvertently rearranging the furniture in my bedroom while the house the band inhabited shook with violent passion, keeping my colleagues entertained, or at least awake, late into the night.

In the months during which we'd worked together, Cheryl Yorkavich and I had developed a friendly, respectful, and completely platonic relationship—I guess I knew she had no interest in me, and so I never tried anything. But in spite of my sexual incontinence she seemed to like me, and I liked her despite the ugly fact that she actually sang *Have You Never Been Mellow* and appeared to en*joy* it. I guess we were just about even. So, on a rare warm afternoon when there was no one around for me to molest, the two of us went to the beach at Seaside Heights to relax and talk and try to get to know each other better.

After basking for a while in the late summer sun, chatting and napping and watching the other sunbathers smolder, we decided to go for a stroll along the beach. Cheryl and I had been walking for just a short time when I glanced toward the water and noticed something. A child was struggling alone against the shallow waves, his tiny pale body vainly battling the undertow. At first it didn't quite register, but then, as the little boy was tugged under, spun, and twisted in the dark, sandy swirl, I lunged in, reached down into the roiling current, and pulled the drenched and shivering child out. He was breathing, but apparently in shock. I turned toward the crowded shore, still holding him at shoulder level, and searched for a parent or someone else to blame. Finally a woman with a blank, unaffected expression pulled his tiny dripping body from me without a word. I had the terrible, nauseating feeling that what I had done, at best, was to delay the inevitable. In spite of all I had seen and done, I guess I was still, in some ways, an innocent.

And early one morning in Tom's River, shortly after Barbara had left for the day, I felt a hand caressing my chest. When I pealed my eyes opened I saw sitting next to me Karla, the other woman who during my first visit to the seemingly magical town of Tom's River had somewhat more discreetly expressed an interest in me. She simply smiled and said, "I heard you guys were back in town, and I wanted to welcome you and tell you that I have something for you if you have any time for me while you're here." What the fuck? I spent my final moist and sticky night in Tom's River with her.

But…

Still hopeful at times, I remained in contact with Carolyn, writing her letters and calling her when I missed her or was in the mood for long distance phone sex, which was more often than I'd like to admit. And she too seemed to be hanging on to something, although it may have simply been that she didn't know how to say goodbye, or that she wanted to keep me available in case no one better came along. Nevertheless, over the following months we would drift farther and farther apart, and I would continue trying to distract myself, supporting my flimsy, undernourished ego with the charitable or mindless assistance of the various women who crossed my winding path.

Fat City Brass was finally dying too. We were becoming bored with each other and probably with ourselves; it was clearly time for everyone to move on. So, having just moved with Mark to a larger, more expensive apartment in Framingham, one of the small suburbs North of Boston on Route 9, I began to search for work again. I did a few auditions and soon found a smaller band that had, over the years, developed a decent reputation around Boston. Within a couple weeks I was playing with, and I am *so* sorry, *Natural Feelin'*.

10

Literally Lousy

Okay. *Natural Feelin'* was a passable top-forty dance band comprised of an above average rhythm section fronted by two adequate, fairly charismatic singers, Debbie Scott and—God, this is embarrassing—Larry Lovejoy. Things began fairly well, but by the end of the final night of my first week, I had threatened to beat Larry, who was now cowering in his car, to a quivering pulp.

Let me explain.

When I walked into our dressing room to change into my civilian attire that night, I found Larry shoving his girlfriend, Donna, around the room. First I calmly let her out of the room. Then I chased Larry down the hall, warning him with apposite profanity of the ugly, painful consequences he would surely suffer if I ever saw him do anything like that again. Larry was a diminutive guy. Otherwise I *might* have behaved much differently. To his credit and my surprise, he did not fire me. In fact, he soon became my friend.

Larry was a tad too slick for me, and he had demonstrated behavior that had always been, and continues to be, unacceptable to me, but—and I know how strange this sounds—but he was otherwise a decent fuck-up. Debbie, our other singer, was nice but a little hard around the edges and a little distant. Pudgy, smiling Val, red-bearded Bo, and cute little Dennis, who looked as though he was lazily sculpted from vanilla pudding, were all fairly bright, amiable, and talented. And, though I never thought I was a particularly good drummer, I was finally beginning to suspect that I added something to any band I was in, both musically and in some other, less tangible areas. My playing seemed, in some way, to challenge the other musicians, forcing them to work harder, and my sense of humor and personality often kept them entertained in between the notes.

Of course there was occasionally some friction; that was inevitable with five sex-crazed young men and one young woman traveling in close quarters and competing for sex, power, laughter, and applause. Nevertheless, under the circumstances, we did quite well most of the time, and sometimes we laughed our little tightly wrapped asses off.

It was while I was playing with *Natural Feelin'* that I did my first sporadic work as a jingle singer and alleged voice-over "artist". Those of you with rich fantasy lives undoubtedly recall my huge vocal hit, "Why spray, when you can vaporize your bugs away?" and my low, authoritative voice as I announced, "Smarten up, New England's *own* wallpaper supermarket."

And it was around that time that I began to actually listen to some of the music I was playing, and to heed the advice and gentle coaching of the other members of the band. Not surprisingly, my playing improved as a consequence. I still didn't really practice or study my instrument in the traditional sense, but I had a good enough ear and enough inherent talent, I suppose, that I was able to erratically progress. Additionally, I found that my increased confidence was reflected in my playing. I learned how important it was to feel comfortable and self-assured in anything I was doing. And as others began to appreciate my wit and humor, I actually became funnier. Hmm.

Before long I was doing most of the announcing, adlibbing whenever I felt the urge, occasionally taking chances that would shock and frighten my coworkers, but which they fully enjoyed nonetheless. I was often just on the edge of offending someone, "Excuse me Miss, would you stop staring at my crotch," but I seldom believed I crossed the line, although one particularly sensitive and emotional Italian-American club owner, "She crossed her legs and broke my sunglasses," was seen standing outside his busy bar on a Friday night, kicking the brick structure repeatedly and swearing to himself that he would "kill that

god-damned-a somunabitch drummer." After that incident our manager put a ban on my microphone privileges, but that didn't last very
long; within weeks I was back at it and we all felt like naughty children,
which, of course, we were. Poo-poo, ca ca.

It was while I was working with *Natural Feelin'* that I received the
unanticipated phone call from Dottie, the tall, curvaceous, unapproachable waitress from the club in Hyannis. It was nine o'clock or
later on my night off when the telephone rang just as I was trying to
devise a new masturbation technique involving a moist wash cloth and
half a gallon of hand lotion. Dottie, who was at a bar with some
friends, asked if I'd like to drive down and have a drink with them. It
would be about an hour's drive, she warned, but she assured me that I
would have a good time. I considered the possibilities and came to the
unprecedented conclusion that if I simply went with the idea of having
fun, rather than feeling that I *had* to get laid, I might actually enjoy
myself. She promised to wait for me and I put my semi-erect penis
away and left immediately, in search of good clean fun.

By the time I arrived at the bar, Dottie and her friends were already
moderately inebriated and having a jolly good time. After introductions, I sat down and another pitcher of beer was immediately poured
and devoured. I felt that I had a responsibility to at least attempt to
catch up with my date, so I increased my drinking speed by approximately fifty percent. Still, no matter how eagerly I partook, she refused
to give up her advantage, and in time the gap actually widened. I was
simply no match for this experienced human sponge.

Had I been alone with her, I don't think I could have done it, but
about an hour later Dottie's two friends helped me cart her lovely lifeless body into my car and then led me to her cozy house near the
beach. It was a long drive, and after we finally got her inside she gradually began to come back to life. When they were convinced she was
going to be all right, her friends left us alone. Dottie asked me to stay
and soon invited me in to her bedroom.

Dottie was still intoxicated, but she knew exactly what she was doing when she looked up at me from her bed and moaned, "I'll do anything you want, anything at all."

Good clean fun.

This was a situation with which I was unfamiliar, and consequently I probably wasn't as creative as a veteran of such circumstances might have been. Nevertheless, it was a stimulating and memorable night, and in the morning I awakened to cool ocean breezes, fresh orange juice, and a delicious homemade breakfast. She was really quite sweet.

Natural Feelin' traveled all around the Northeast, and I continued to make new friends, trying to obscure my lingering sadness under foreign sheets, between unfamiliar thighs. There must have been dozens of fetching women who wandered unaware into my greedy arms and in whom I fleetingly buried myself and my urgent desperation. I laughed a lot, and fucked and sucked a growing group of unwary strangers while Larry and I competed to see who could waste more of his hard-earned money on unsightly clothing. I thank God there are no remaining photographs to document my poor taste. Oh yeah, and the band had spiffy new outfits that were designed and constructed by some sadistic musician-hating seamstress: tight white polyester pants and pullover tops with long strings of shiny snap-on sequins, the backs of which were sharp enough to take a sizeable core sample from any flesh they sunk their steely teeth into. Dear God.

Somewhere in all of this confusion and embarrassment I met a young woman from Quincy. On our second date she told me about her brutally sadistic boyfriend. She had been trying to leave him for months, she explained. But whenever she gathered the nerve to tell him she was going, he would threaten, quite convincingly, to hurt or kill her. The last time she'd attempted an escape, he came to her house and abducted her, escorting her back to the house where he lived with his parents, where he tethered her to his bed. He kept her there in full view of his indifferent parents for over a week, bringing her food and water when he felt she deserved it, and mutilating her with cigarettes and razor blades when he was in a less generous mood. She had been in hiding, and terribly afraid, since her most recent late-night getaway. She was very sad and very nice and I simply couldn't bring myself to take advantage of her. I told her I was still in love with Carolyn (which may well have been true) and that I couldn't see her any more. I think I hurt her, but hopefully less than I might have had I been less honest. Who the hell knows?

And there was the wealthy lass in Albany who afflicted me with a condition that would quickly become the cause of much concern and more than a little scratching and squirming. I had never before experienced an intimate infestation, and I was first frightened out of my wits, and then deeply humiliated. I remember, after days of steadily increasing but still unexplained discomfort, reaching down and capturing one of the thousand or so evil fanged demons between my trembling thumb and forefinger. I squeezed it tightly enough to crush a fresh walnut and then reached over to switch on the light by my bed, but when I pealed my nervous digits open the vile biting bastard leapt onto my bed. I let out a terrifying shriek as it disappearing into the shadowy safety of the blankets.

Dizzy and covered with sweat, my heart pummeling my chest, I sprinted to the bathroom. Frantically, I filled the tub with steaming water, poured out a bottle of shampoo and some rubbing alcohol, and immersed myself into the scalding, redolent brew. I tried drowning them, I poured Listerine over their stomping grounds, triggering an uncomfortable burning in my already maligned genitals; I tried detergents, cleaning fluids, orange juice, ice cubes, Coke, shaving cream, and virtually anything I could find. I was, for an insane moment, sorely tempted by the Drano that sat next to the toilet, but after a minute's consideration I wisely controlled that impulse.

Early the next morning, after a long night of frenzied, clandestine research, I made my way to the nearest drug store, where I shyly waited for a male clerk to help me before purchasing a bottle of A-200. I rushed home and assailed the hostile vermin with bloody murder in my heart. I shampooed and scrubbed and rubbed myself raw while everything I owned, every sheet and blanket, every pair of pants and underwear, everything that could fit into a washing machine went through endless cycles on the "Volcanic lava" temperature setting before baking in the oven at 450 degrees for over an hour or until golden brown. I washed and washed again with a violent, deadly, single-minded passion, and yes, I destroyed those horrid, itching, biting fiends. I wanted nothing more than to kill the young woman in Albany. But I was not about to get that close again without a tanker truck full of A-200 and an airtight rubber suit.

11

The Curse

Then in Framingham there was the shy anorexic waitress I liked very much but did not sleep with, or even kiss with open lips. And at the Somerville Holiday Inn I encountered Judy Pantino, a petite, gentle woman, who was unhappily married to a man who apparently didn't have the patience, interest, or capacity to please her. Judy was the first uncarpeted woman I ever molested, but after the concerns aroused by my recent painful and demoralizing experience with those verminous denizens of the insect kingdom, I was delighted to be able to investigate the neighborhood unhampered before risking my comfort and my health. Is that so wrong?

Sadly, Judy's sexuality was inhibited by a rigid, guilt-inducing Catholic upbringing. Intercourse, for her, was tainted by a feeling of shame, and consequently it required time and patience to satisfy her sexually. My jaw may never fully recover from our marathon sessions, but Judy was always appreciative, and she was quite dear.

One night, long after I'd decoded her complex pleasure system and we'd gotten to know each other fairly well, Judy timidly confessed to me an as yet unrealized intimate fantasy. She told me that though she would certainly never want to be raped, she wouldn't mind at all if some night someone she trusted were to take her by force; she theorized that this might somehow assuage her deeply ingrained Catholic guilt and enable her to more easily enjoy the art of intercourse. I said I wasn't sure I could comply, but that if she really wanted me to, I would consider it and possibly surprise her one night.

When she visited my apartment the following week, we shared a bottle of wine in my small eat-in kitchen before moving toward the bedroom. I fought my instincts for a minute before wrestling her down onto my bed. Unfortunately, she landed a little harder than I'd intended. I asked her if she was okay and she smiled up at me and nodded. Clumsily, I dropped down on top of her and tore her blouse open, hoping I had somewhere in my apartment a needle and thread with which to refasten her buttons before sending her home to her husband. Pinning her down on the bed, I held both of her tiny wrists together with one hand. She moaned and I asked her if I had hurt her and she shook her head. I rolled her over and roughly pulled her panties down along with her jeans; she fought back a little and I asked her if she wanted me to stop, if she was all right. When she said no we both began to laugh at my ineptitude. I simply couldn't bear the thought of hurting her. I didn't have the capacity to be quite that barbaric, and I suspect we both liked me a little more because of it. Oh well.

The next stop for *Natural Feelin'* was Waterbury, Connecticut. And it was in that town that my constantly evolving comedy routine, an increasingly raunchy commingling of tired old jokes and irreverent but frequently inspired adlibbing, expanded to virtually consume a forty-minute set.

Playing in Waterbury was like drifting backward in time; the entire community, from the storefronts to the hairdos to the clothing, seemed stuck in the nineteen-fifties. And although I met a couple tempting women there, I had no success whatsoever, which may have been because from their vantage point I was already wearing the worst of the clothing from the future. From Waterbury we fled to Buffalo, where we played for two weeks before heading to Cleveland and The Final Approach, a flashy nightclub on the top floor of a large modern hotel near the airport that we referred to only as "The Anal Approach."

Although the band was staying there in the hotel, it usually wasn't until early afternoon that we straggled down, one or two at a time, to the coffee shop, where a comely and frustratingly pure, corn-fed Midwestern girl served us breakfast. I flirted with Debbie and she flirted coyly with me, and she gave me quite a few meals at no charge. At the beginning of our second week Debbie invited me to her parents' ranch, where their "best horse" tried to dismember me, charging across an open field and leaping over a cliff before coming to a terrifying and excruciatingly painful halt. Debbie and I exchanged cautious affection and called each other sweet names, but she was a virgin and planned to remain one for as long as she lived. I suspect the horse was in on the loathsome scheme.

Late in our stay in Cleveland, aware of my unprecedented carnal penury, Larry took the initiative, approaching two women we'd both noticed in the audience. After only a few minutes, he called me over and introduced me to them, and soon we were sitting together exchanging pleasantries while silently choosing our mates. The next night I went home with the one I chose, or who chose me, or who was left after one of the other two chose the other one of the other two. My long dry season had finally come to an end. The curse was broken.

During the joyous week that followed I spent most of my nights testing my equipment and cleaning my pipes with my new victim. And every day without fail Larry reminded me that he'd been instrumental in ending the imprecation. He was certain that I owed him something, at least an enthusiastic "thank you," for having introduced me to this most recent target of my venery. And I continued eating breakfast in the hotel restaurant, not merely because the food was often free, but because I was still quite fond of the virgin Debbie. Although it was clear that her feelings were hurt when she learned of the other, more agreeable, or simply less cautious woman, she still treated me kindly. Inexplicably, she seemed to almost understand. Or maybe she simply didn't like me *that* much.

The band's next booking was at a glitzy newly-opened hotel in Wilkes-Barre, Pennsylvania, only fifty miles from where my mother still lived, and less than a mile from the massive shopping mall where Larry and I would spend (and spend) every free afternoon. And while we purchased a boatload of hideous new polyester garments, he continued to demand the show of appreciation he felt certain he was owed.

Toward the end of the second week of our three-week stay in Wilkes-Barre, the girls from Cleveland, who, unbeknownst to us, had secured two rooms in a less expensive nearby hotel, paid us a visit. After Larry and I finished work on the night of their unexpected appearance, the four of us went out to Denny's, where we had a late night snack before retiring to their separate rooms. An hour or so later I called Larry's room and asked him to leave the phone off the hook, and though he had no idea what to expect, he reluctantly complied. Later, as I was coming, I grabbed the telephone and screamed into the receiver, "Thank you Larry." I'm certain my date, who'd come so far to see me, was overcome by waves of tender affection. Oh, what a joy I must have been.

12

Dishonorable Discharge

Several weeks and half a dozen women later, back in Massachusetts, I had another uncomfortable and frightening sensation in or around the area of my haggard groin. Had the woman from Cleveland exacted revenge? "Painful urination" is the phrase I silently rehearsed before finally searching out a VD clinic. As it turned out, there was a clinic conveniently located at Framingham hospital, so all I had to do was drive for five minutes, step out of my car, and shrivel with unbearable shame and embarrassment before going inside.

As I skulked through the hospital's main entrance, I spied an elderly woman sitting behind a wide wooden desk and providing information to those who were lost, confused, or just plain stupid. For a few minutes I wandered around the halls near the entrance, waiting for the right time to approach the grinning woman. Finally, when there was no one else in sight, I slithered over to her desk, leaned close, and whispered, "Hi, can you tell me how to get to the VD clinic?"

"Excuse me?" She squinted and bent forward, creaking.

"I'm looking for the VD clinic," I said timidly.

"Speak up, son."

I peered around and noticed that a small crowd had materialized. Moving close enough to lick her pasty face, I bellowed, "How—do—I—get—to—the," then in a frustrated whisper directed carefully at her fuzzy off-white ear drum, "VD clinic?"

With a satanic sneer she glared at me and shouted, "OH, YOU WANT THE **VD** CLINIC." My heart raced as her voice echoed through the corridors. "WELL THE **VD** CLINIC IS RIGHT

DOWN THAT HALL ON YOUR LEFT. YOU'LL SEE A BIG
SIGN ON THE DOOR THAT SAYS **VD** IN BRIGHT RED LET-
TERS. THAT STANDS FOR **VENEREAL DISEASE** YOUNG
MAN. IS THAT WHAT YOU HAVE? **SOME**
VENEREAL DISEASE?"

With my head down, I raced blindly through the bright white corridors for what seemed like an hour. Finally, my heart still thumping
wildly, I approached the door and stepped into the waiting room,
where I sat down and pondered where I might wish to live now that all
of New England was aware of my suspected affliction. I watched as my
fellow sufferers, looking gloomy and dejected, trudged one by one into
the small office, and then as they ultimately emerged, looking even
more forlorn. Silently, I prayed that the doctor, at least, would not be a
woman.

Soon enough my name was called, and I was ushered into a smaller
room, where I sat alone, cataloging, just for the record, all of the good
I'd done in my life. I'd just finished going over the brief list a second
time when a tall and truly beautiful woman entered the room. She sat
down next to me and causally put her feet up on the bottom drawer of
her filing cabinet as she organized the papers on her clipboard.

"Hi Grant," she said, and glanced up at me. "What seems to be the
problem?"

"I've been experiencing some…uh, some pain."

"Any particular area, Grant?"

"You're not going to make this easy for me, are you?"

She laughed, "Okay, is it after you urinate?"

"Yes, I'm afraid it is. Is that…bad?"

"Any other symptoms?"

"Well, I don't know if this is related or not, but I find myself desperately wishing I were anywhere else but here, and that if I absolutely *had*
to be here, which I apparently do, that you could be a senile old man
with schnauzer breath and failing vision."

"Sounds serious."

"Ya *think?*"

She inquired about my allergies and my past medical history, and finally about my sexual history. She seemed somewhat impressed, and I thought for a moment about asking her out, but fortunately realized how foolish that would be. After finishing her paperwork, she sent me in to see the doctor.

The physician was probably not an evil man; I suppose it could even be argued that he was just doing his job. But after extracting a relatively painless blood sample, he assumed an alarming expression and ordered me to drop my pants and underwear. For some insane reason, despite every warning instinct, I nervously complied. Then he motioned to a cold metal table, where I sat and spread my legs as he unsheathed the most revolting invention I have ever seen. The twisted metal handle was narrow and about a foot long, and at the business end was the sharp, thickly bristled brush with which he was now threatening to gore me. If I'd had a gun I would have emptied it on him immediately and without remorse. He told me to relax and I laughed morbidly and then fell into a state of shock as he seized my terrified and flaccid member and thrust the homicidal contraption all the fucking way through my fucking tormented penis into my fucking brain and out my fucking screaming asshole. I was on fire. I didn't look down. I *couldn't* look down, and yet I'm certain the inhumane son-of-a-bitch twisted and jerked and spun the barbed bristles from hell as my bulging eyes filled with tears and my pulse shot up to double anaerobic. Finally, with a depraved grunt, he tugged his weapon out of mine and the world went silent and black. I collapsed as my sinuses cleared. My sinuses are still clear. They'll be clear when I'm dead. I knew I would never have sex again; even if I was eventually able to, it simply wasn't worth it.

A week later, still dizzy from the pain, I returned to the scene of my execution. I sprinted past the deaf woman (who undoubtedly recognized me as that young man with **"SOME VENERIAL DISEASE"**) and found my own way back to the abattoir, where I met once again with the friendly young woman. She informed me that I had a clear bill of health, that my symptoms had, in her opinion, most likely been caused by "extreme overuse." She actually giggled when she said it. The diagnosis? A weary pee-pee. After suggesting that I slow down a little, she sent me skulking home with my tail between my legs. I had the subtle sense that a date was probably out of the question.

13

Love Letters and Doggie Darts

A short time after my grisly ordeal at the clinic, my roommate, Mark, moved back to Pennsylvania, leaving me to find my own, more humble lodging. Although my new apartment, which was closer to Framingham's quiet downtown area, was not as modern as the one I'd shared with Mark, it was mine nonetheless, and it was probably time for me to finally learn to live alone anyway. But because the large color television and the nice furniture to which I'd become accustomed had all belonged to Mark, I was left without some creature comforts. And while I missed those luxuries, I learned very quickly to appreciate my time alone and the freedom to act out without the fear of any judgments but my own, which were always too lenient or too harsh.

I remember regularly coming home late at night and downing half a box of Breyer's chocolate ice cream while watching old movies on the four-inch black and white television Jackie had given me for my birthday years before. I remember having Judy and various other unfortunates over to spend at least part of the night, and I recall missing and sometimes telephoning Carolyn, whose loss I still seemed unable or unwilling to fully accept.

Nevertheless, I gradually made some new friends, and, at least for a while, exercised greater caution in terms of my venereal health. And Larry and I intensified our concomitant competitions for repulsive apparel and attractive women while the band traversed New England from Maine to Upstate New York.

It was toward the end of what would turn out to be our last road-trip together that we found ourselves back in Waterbury, Connecticut.

And it was from that anachronistic town that the first, and possibly the only amorous bulk mailing was dispatched.

One afternoon, when Debbie was absent and the rest of us were relaxing in one of the hotel rooms alternately bragging and grousing about the women in our lives, I had what seemed at the time like a flash of inspiration. I suggested to my colleagues that we compose a form letter disclosing to the assorted objects of our love or lust how much we missed them. After eagerly rounding up enough writing implements and hotel stationery to satisfy our needs, I dictated a generic love letter. And that evening on the way to the club I mailed a fistful of epistles, identical outside of the names, to the various women we loved or missed or just wanted to be certain we could fuck again as soon as we returned home.

Only after mailing these almost heartfelt missives did it occur to me that I might, in all the idiotic laughter and confusion, have inadvertently placed the letter intended for "A" in the envelope addressed to "B," or vice-versa. For over a week I lived in dread, but if I *did* make an error no one ever mentioned it. Yes, it was a cruel trick, but we meant no real harm; the idea just seemed so damned funny at the time. And anyway, it was a good and apparently effective letter. Everyone got laid, several with what was described as "uncharacteristic enthusiasm."

But *Natural Feelin'* was coming to its natural end. Our final engagement was a two-week stint at the Holiday Inn in Somerville, Massachusetts, where the staff and customers alike knew us well, and where felt perfectly at ease acting like the bunch of out of control fucking assholes that at times we truly were.

So...

One restless night as we were stumbling out of the hotel lounge, Larry and I decided we weren't quite drunk enough yet to drown in our own vomit, so we went to his house in Boston's outskirts to drink tequila and reminisce about the band that was dying and our numerous exploits together. After an hour or so of heavy drinking and juvenile laughter, Larry suggested a game of darts. I'd never played the game before, but he announced that he was quite competent, and offered to allow me a handicap of several hundred points. After hanging the circular board on the narrow section of wall that separated his living room from his dining room, Larry patiently demonstrated the proper technique, showing me how to stand, how to hold the darts, and how to throw, while we poured back repeated sticky, burning shots of tequila.

When it was finally time for me to toss my first dart I felt fairly well prepared. Standing up as straight as I could, I pulled back my right arm, and with confidence borne of blinding inebriation I let the perfectly balanced metal-tipped missile fly. It whistled briskly past the board, missed the wall completely, and continued its brief trajectory, disappearing into the inky blackness of the living room. A split second later, there was a dull thud, which was followed by a high-pitched yelp. For a second, Larry and I just stared at each other. Then, as quickly as was possible given our shared temulency, we staggered into the living room. His poor dog was stretched out across the floor, gazing sadly up at us with the feathered wooden projectile jutting from the furry flesh around his ribs like the flag of a conquering nation of fleas.

Larry leaned down to pull the inadvertent weapon out, and the dog, who would thereafter be known as "Bull's-eye," howled before jumping up and marching briskly away. Only when he'd reached the theoretical safety of the kitchen did he turn to glare back at me and snarl.

I have always loved the higher animals, and I'd like to think I've done my best to protect them from those who would think to harm them. But I could not stop laughing, and neither could Larry, whose beloved beast I had pierced. But I would never pick up a dart again without bloody murder in my heart.

And…

On our final night at the Holiday Inn, inappropriately comfortable in the awareness that we would never be coming back, we were completely out of control. I did the worst and most offensive of my comedy, "Somebody threw a rock through the window and hit her in the tit, breaking three of my fingers," and we swore and drank and attacked ruthlessly everyone in our paths. And for some reason I'll never understand, almost everyone seemed to enjoy the insanity, with the possible exception of the bouncer, upon whose jacket, Larry, his back courteously turned to the audience, urinated.

There was something very liberating about knowing we could say and do whatever we wanted without the fear that it might come back to haunt us the following week or month. There was nothing these people could do to hurt me; I would never see any of them again.

Well...

Until I joined *Ruby*, a band based in Denver but working at that time around Boston. Our first job, just two weeks later, was at the very familiar Holiday Inn at Somerville.

Oops.

14

I Like Television

Ruby was a better band than any I had played with to that point. Kim and Phyllis, two proficient, well-proportioned singers, performed in front of a powerful and incredibly tight rhythm section skillfully supported by a bright, competent, too tall, too handsome light and sound technician. Provoked by necessity and inspiration, my own musical skills rapidly improved, and although I still lacked confidence, I began to occasionally find a hint of pleasure in playing music. We were not a mainstream top-forty band; we played music most bands at the time would never have attempted, and we played it relatively well, I think. Outside of the stabbing fear brought on by a few mock threats from the bouncer, who was sporting a lovely new unscented jacket (on which I complimented him repeatedly), I was reasonably comfortable back in Somerville.

And I was happy with my new band. They were gifted musicians and nice enough people, and they seemed to like me, though once again I was constrained to prance around in a bizarre array of shiny, 'rock and roll' outfits, at least one of which offered visual access to my tiny twenty-six inch midriff. How embarrassing.

The next stop for *Ruby* was the delightful and stimulating slum of Buffalo, New York, where we inhabited the same dingy roadside motel as *Sunrise*, another, larger Denver-based band with whom we also shared a management agency. In addition to the slightly more accessible music they played, *Sunrise* focused heavily on comedy and showmanship. Nancy, the more notable of the band's two female singers, and a former "Miss Montana," was an exceptionally alluring, slender, dark-haired she-beast.

Not surprisingly, I pursued Nancy, even after receiving the admonition that Bill, their soundman, was deeply in love with her and might be quite likely to murder anyone who got in the way of his as yet unrequited ardor. By the time we left Buffalo I knew I had at least made an impression; though we hadn't slept together, she had indulged me with a moist and very intimate goodbye kiss in my car on their final day there. Nancy remained in my mind and in my fantasies for quite a while, and for a time we exchanged occasional correspondence. It was easy to imagine falling in love with her, but in terms of proximity Bill had a definite advantage, at least for the moment. Still, I had a hopeful sense that I might run into her in Denver, our next destination.

I'd never before been to Colorado, and I still remember the childlike excitement I felt as I steered my rattling red Datsun across the endless plains of Nebraska, the huge, snowcapped mountains gradually rising up before me like giant gray-humped dinosaurs. I journeyed west with some illusions that I suppose are not terribly uncommon. I envisaged Denver as a beautiful, unsoiled city, surrounded by mountains and as safe and friendly as any small country town. The people would be neighborly, the air fresh and clean.

There were mountains.

Our initial booking in Denver was at a shabby downtown club, where on the first break of our first night a young man approached me at the bar and enthusiastically offered to show me his glass eye. Before I had time to decline his offer, I was gazing into an empty socket under an arched brow while his eye stared blankly back at me from the palm of his dark, sweaty hand. Yummy. Look into my palm.

And late one night that same week, after I had retired to my room to read, Phyllis, whose room was just across the hall, stopped in to tell me how much she enjoyed working with me and to say goodnight. I thanked her and wished her a good night before returning to my book. For a minute she remained at the foot of my bed. Seconds later, to my eternal surprise, a dozen tiny snaps popped and her housedress fell open, revealing a pale but well-formed figure. I'm not sure I can explain my failure to act; maybe my brain somehow kicked in before my penis had a chance to respond, but for some reason, I simply continued reading. *Ruby* worked in and around Denver for another month or so, and I, demonstrating uncharacteristic wisdom, kept a safe distance from Phyllis, who fortunately never repeated her striptease—for me at least. And it was never mentioned. Oh…until now.

The band continued to improve, and I continued to grow as a musician, if not as a human being. We gradually developed a small but faithful following in Denver, but there was still some doubt about our ability to keep the grumbling club owners happy. Our audience, despite their enthusiasm, was limited, and many of the regulars in the various clubs in which we played were only interested in hearing music they'd heard a thousand times before played the way they were used to hearing it. Thump, thump, thump. Isn't that what radios are for? Although we were determined to hang on and enjoy our minor success for as long as we could, I think we all realized that the band, such as it was, wouldn't survive for terribly long.

From Denver *Ruby* traveled south to Pueblo, where we played at a very upscale, very fashionable, newly opened club called, Furphy's. Furphy's was owned and managed by a somehow odd, but quite pleasant man, coincidentally named Fritz Furphy. During the day my roommate Glenn and I explored the dry, dusty city, and at night, as we played to a devoted crowd, I scanned the audience for prey. Fritz, who was quite fond of our band, would regularly invite us to sit and drink tequila with him after hours in the empty club. And we rarely declined.

Early in our stay I came close, I think, to seducing a tall, attractive young woman who was visiting Pueblo with an old man in some mysterious arrangement that I never *did* decipher. But in the end she was unwilling, with me at least, although for all I know the wrinkly old bastard was having his filthy way with her every night—a thought that truly disgusted me then and still does and probably will until I am a wrinkly old bastard praying for someone as kind and open-minded or as venal and immoral as she presumably was.

During our second week at Furphy's I met an interesting, slightly older woman who seemed to like me, but who, with shy apologies, went home alone every night. We kissed a little and once I even went back to her apartment with her, but still I ended up in my room at our hotel every night, unsatisfied and alone. It wasn't until the end of the week that she informed me that although she wanted to make love with me, there was a minor problem. She promised to explain her cryptic comment "someday" and I left Pueblo confused and frustrated. It wasn't that I had any special fondness for, or even a powerful attraction to this woman, it was just that I couldn't have what I thought I might possibly want. Poor baby.

I was back in Denver when, a week later, she called me and asked me if I would like to come down and spend the night with her. Despite my ambivalence, I decided to go; after all, I had work to complete.

When I arrived at her apartment she was waiting with a smile and dinner was cooking. Her son, she explained, was staying with his father. After a quiet dinner we retired to her living room, where I sipped a glass of red wine while she sat across from me drinking water and describing the rare but potentially fatal heart condition that kept her from enjoying life as fully as she would have liked.

She said that although it might not be outwardly apparent, she was actually a very sick woman. Her illness was one that could be life threatening if she wasn't extremely cautious and hyper-vigilant. She went on to explain that it was imperative that she take her medications regularly and avoid "any type of excitement." There was the risk of permanent damage to her heart every time she became excited. Exercise or even fear might endanger or shorten her life. This, she told me, was the reason she had avoided anything more potentially stimulating than a gentle kiss. I wasn't certain what to do or say; it even occurred to me that this might be a particularly creative excuse for avoiding a sexual encounter—the clever female equivalent to "My penis was shot off in

Vietnam." But after our disconcerting discussion she came over and took my hand, led me into her bedroom, and said, "I want to make love."

"What about your heart?" I asked, confused and a little frightened, my voice a mousy squeak.

"Well," she said. "If we're careful, and I don't become too excited, it will *probably* be okay."

Probably.

"You know, we don't have to do this," I stuttered. "We can just sit and talk about something; we can watch some television. I *like* television." But while I was nervously proclaiming my fondness for the wonders of television, she was quietly undressing and preparing the bed—or coffin.

Standing before me in her underwear, she looked at me and said, "I want to make love. It's been a long time."

Reluctantly, I undressed and got into her bed, hoping, for the first and last time in my life, that I wouldn't be a very good lover.

And I'm fairly certain I wasn't. There is a limit to how aroused one can get while waiting for his partner to croak. Every moan, every groan, every heavy breath was a warning to me to stop doing whatever it was that was giving her pleasure. Counter to all of my instincts, a voice inside me was silently, repeatedly screaming, "Please, *please* don't have an orgasm." It was an awkward, passionless act of deadly kindness, and, as sorry as I felt for this woman whose name I have long since forgotten, I never returned. I kept in touch with her for a short time from a safe distance, but there was something awful about what I had done, and I knew I couldn't do it again, even though I knew too that not going back was probably just as awful. Sometimes the right choice is not so clear. Sometimes, maybe there *is* no right choice.

And then…

In Denver we played at a new club, where we were mostly well received and where I continued my ceaseless fanatical search for new talent. One night, as I sat behind my drums, I noticed two women sitting together at a table near the dance floor. Occasionally, one or the other of them would get up and dance with one of a series of goobers who approached them, and each time I would smile, silently, but manifestly criticizing their dance partners and promoting my own insidious agenda. And they played along, covertly laughing at these poor unwitting clowns as I alternately mocked and flirted.

After our third set one of the alluring women motioned to me to join them at their table. They offered me a drink and for a few minutes the three of us chatted. Soon they explained that they were both happily married to musicians, and that the two of them often went out together while their respective mates were working. They were happy, they said, to meet a guy who wasn't just trying to get laid. And I told them, mostly sincerely, that it was reassuring to meet two women who were satisfied with their marriages and uninterested in other men. I explained that I'd had one or two relationships with married women and had begun to wonder if anyone was faithful any more. That, at least, was true.

It was an interesting situation. The self-induced pressure to be charming and to evoke a response was relieved. I could be myself without trying too hard. Consequently, I enjoyed our conversation so much that I didn't want to let them go when the band had finished for the night. As it turned out, they felt the same way. They offered to drive me home, an offer that, tossing my car keys to Phyllis, I cheerfully accepted.

But then...

On the way out of the club that night, one of the women asked me if I would like to smoke a joint with them. I declined, but said I'd be happy to just hang out with them while they got high. So I sat between the two loyal wives in the front seat of their car while they passed the glowing joint back and forth in front of me. We talked and we laughed and I couldn't decide whether to feel good about their allegiance to their husbands or to bemoan their unavailability to me until I noticed a slight pressure on my left thigh. A friendly gesture, I thought, and a second hand found my right knee in the darkness. As the conversation progressed, the two independent hands, each one's owner apparently unaware of the stealthy movements of the other, began to slide slowly crotchward©. My feelings at this moment were confused and contradictory. The good news: these women were both attracted to me, and evidently willing to act on that attraction. The bad news: they weren't the faithful wives I had come to believe they were, and, more importantly, at the rate their hands were traveling, they were going to meet in the middle within minutes. If I was right, and neither was aware of the furtive actions of the other, there was the potential for a very uneasy, if humorous moment. In spite of my powerful instincts, when they were both within centimeters of my growing, humming, widely grinning penis (sorry), I decided to put both of my hands on theirs, hoping to protect them from the embarrassment that would surely follow there unexpected meeting. But I was too late. Their fingers met and they both shrieked, then laughed nervously while my chances of an intimate adventure with either of these two lovely young liars dissolved before my tired eyes. In awkward silence, they drove me home, and we all laughed uneasily before parting forever. I was deeply depressed.

It was probably 1975, and the band, as good as it was, was at its end. The general population wasn't interested in good music played well, or at least that was my story, and my life was about to change once again. Thump, thump, thump.

15

School Daze

Remember *Sunrise*, the other band from Denver, the one I met when we were playing in Buffalo, the one the delicious Miss Montana was in? Yep, they suddenly found themselves in need of a new drummer. Although the music wasn't likely to be as interesting or as challenging as it had been with *Ruby*, they were a decent band, and I was enticed by the potential for an opportunity to express some of my alleged comic talents. Unfortunately, *Sunrise* was working at a club in Northern Massachusetts when I was hired, which meant I was forced to tackle that horrible two-thousand-mile drive in my clanking old Datsun once again. But the prospect of a new adventure and Nancy were waiting at the other end, along with an assortment of hideous multi-colored double-knit suits. It is truly a miracle that I *ever* got laid.

Nancy looked great and sang reasonably well, but I never understood why Kathy, the band's other female vocalist, had been hired. She was dull, awkward, and a little manly on stage, and her voice was harsh and grating. As far as I could tell her only vaguely salable feature was a sclapful of blond hair, the problem with which was that it was on *her* oversized head, which was perched directly over *her* pale and lumpy body. I'm sure she is a lovely human being. Ron, a devout alcoholic, played keyboards, sax, and valve trombone; Ed, who according to reports the source of which was never clear, had a huge penis, played trumpet and valve trombone; Harper played guitar and trombone, and Steve played bass. Everyone sang, for better and for worse. And as if that wasn't enough, John operated the lights and Bill did the sound. And, eventually, Nancy. Bastard.

When I arrived at the club in Massachusetts and unloaded my tiny, too sparkly "jazz" drum set, the other band members frowned in unison. One fatuous theory in circulation at that time was that the more equipment you possessed, the better you must be; someone actually asked where the rest of my set was. "In the store," was my dust-dry retort. Nevertheless, after their initial concerns were allayed by my relative competence on my dinky little kit, I was quickly and enthusiastically accepted by all—with the possible exception of Bill, who, regardless of the fact that he viewed me as a competitor, *was* surprisingly nice to me.

Though I wasn't terribly excited about some of the music they played, *Sunrise* was new and different for me, and they'd cultivated a huge following in the Northeast, which meant regular work and the likelihood of meeting a great variety of potential new victims—and spending time in or around Nancy.

But...

Sadly, my hopes for a romance with Nancy were brutally shattered when Bill approached me early one evening and asked if we could, at my convenience, have a private discussion. When we were both finished working that night, I met Bill at the bar. I bought him a conciliatory beer, and the two of us stood there for a few minutes drinking in tense silence. When he finally began to speak, Bill explained that he was very much in love with Nancy, adding with diffident confidence that he believed she was finally beginning to care for him too. He was aware of my interest in her, and concerned that I might get in the way of their budding relationship. Generously, he admitted that Nancy was fond of me, and he asked me, in the gentlest way possible, to be considerate of his feelings and to allow him the opportunity to pursue the woman he loved, unobstructed. It would have been very difficult for anyone with a heart or a brain to deny his calm and very direct appeal. It would have been difficult even for me. Bill and I became good friends while I kept a frustrated, respectful distance from Nancy. Fucker.

Before leaving New England for Canada, we lost Harper to another, more rock oriented band. We immediately replaced him with a sweet, young, innocent, longhaired guitar player from Boston, and, in the process, added to my dubious involvement in the vocals and comedy.

And…

From Toronto we journeyed to Buffalo, where I met a cute young woman in the club in which we were playing, who after spending the night with me asked me if I could drop her off at school. She meant—and I swear I had no clue until I saw all the big yellow buses dispensing giggling little boys and girls—high school. Oops. From Buffalo we escaped in the dark of night to Cincinnati, where I met Jeannie, who was well over fifteen.

16

Double Dating

Jeannie was slender and athletic, with long, straight blond hair, vivid blue eyes, and a biting sense of humor. Night after night I watched in awe as she effortlessly fended off the incessant advances of her drooling pursuers, leaving them emotionally scarred and bloodied across the bar. Because of this I flirted shyly and cautiously at first, watching and waiting for the inevitable assault, but when it did not come I decided I had to act. I knew what might happen, but I was willing to risk whatever dignity and self respect I might have in the interest of possibly spending some time alone with this beautiful, charmingly caustic woman.

When I finally gathered the nerve to ask her out she consented, and we agreed to get together at some undetermined time later that week. But there was a problem. I was experiencing some mild but worsening symptoms, uncomfortably similar to those I'd suffered before my painful visit to the Framingham torture chamber and the nefarious Doctor Rip Yercockoff.

I was torn, so to speak. I obviously couldn't sleep with Jeannie without being certain I was healthy, but the thought of another such test was enough to forever extirpate my capacity or desire to incite a useful erection. It was possible, even likely that she had no interest in a sexual relationship with me, but if she *was* interested, or if I could trick her into thinking she was, as I so dearly hoped, I couldn't risk infecting her, and an honest explanation could easily have extinguished any tiny flames I might have unknowingly ignited. "I'm sorry," I tried to imagine myself saying. "I can't sleep with you right now because I have a

nasty case of syphilis with a side order of gonorrhea, but if you're willing to wait the month or so until my dick stops burning and spewing
thick green slime and I'm cured to come see me wherever I am at that
time, I'd *love* to fuck you and maybe even get to know you a little bit
better." I may have been wrong, but that just didn't sound like something to which most women would respond with lustful caresses.

So the following morning I dragged myself out of bed before the
crack of noon to scour the phone book for clinics. When that was
unsuccessful I telephoned a local hospital, where before hanging up in
unconcealed disgust, the petulant health care professional chastised me
for even mentioning the disgraceful scourge of venereal disease. It was
Ron who, after learning of my frantic penile plight, came to my rescue.
He explained with remarkable calm that he'd been to hundreds of clinics in at least forty-three states and that he was overdue for his regular
check-up. And just a couple hours later, Ron and I sat in a crowded
waiting room laughing like nervous boy scouts as we awaited the terrible shaft of doom.

I will spare you the grisly details—this time—except to say that I
fainted.

The following evening, when I approached the bar, Jeannie greeted
me with a smile. She leaned close and asked if this would be a good
night for me. I said that if I understood her question correctly it would
be a wonderful night.

So…

After work that night, in separate cars, we drove to the nearby
Denny's, where we sat for hours, eating pancakes and eggs and discussing life, love, ethics, and morality. It was probably four o'clock in the
morning when in the dark Denny's parking lot I finally gave her a gentle goodnight kiss. Jeannie thanked me sweetly before getting into her
clunky white dodge and driving off.

The subsequent day seemed endless—I was eager and afraid. Nevertheless, as soon as I arrived at the club that night I made my way to the
bar and asked her if she would like to go out with me again. When she

said yes, I told her the good news. It was my birthday. What I did not tell her, at that point, was that the results from my tests had come back negative, and that if she wanted me to, I would be happy to indulge her in hours of passionate but tender fucking and sucking. She must have figured out that last part all by herself.

It was sometime in the afternoon, and Ed was sitting on his bed reading a magazine, when I limped into my hotel room the following day. He just glanced up at me for a second and said, "You look like shit," and then, looking back down at his book, "Jesus, you smell like a vagina." I thanked him before drifting happily to sleep.

Jeannie was a fascinating, intelligent woman, and it wasn't difficult, in the subsequent days and nights, to fall terminally in love with her. Do you think I had a problem? What was amazing was that she fell in love with me too. I was a happy man. I'd somehow discovered (in Ohio no less) a very special, very passionate woman—a woman who made it much easier for me to finally forget, or at least put into perspective, the pain of losing Carolyn. And we both tried hard, in the lonely days following my reluctant departure, to sustain the feelings we'd summoned, writing regularly and speaking on the telephone every day.

The band was playing at a Ramada Inn in Cape Cod when Jeannie flew up to see me the following week. And as we became closer and more familiar with one another we grew more comfortable and trusting. In spite of our inherent insecurities, we shared intimacies neither of us had ever shared before. Late one night in our tiny cabin in Hyannisport, Jeannie said she had a "friend" she wanted me to meet. I had to lie facedown on the bed while she made mysterious rustling sounds behind me. Tense minutes later a slightly altered voice with a thick southern drawl sighed, "Hi honey, I've heard a lot about you." And perched on the edge of the bed, wearing a dark wig, a low-cut, black negligee, and very high heals, was Jeannie's truck-stop-waitress alter ego, "Betty Sue."

The strangely familiar woman told me how much she'd envied Jeannie, and how eager she had been to meet me, and I responded with nervous appreciation as she moved closer and placed a strangely familiar hand on my thigh. This was a new and not entirely comfortable experience for me, but I did my best to play along, realizing as it was happening, that this was one intriguing way to sleep with another woman without technically being unfaithful. Bonus! We made love (a little awkwardly), and afterwards I looked over at her and asked, "Did you *both* come?" We all laughed hard until their wig fell off.

Notwithstanding my initial confusion at the unexpected manifestation of her imaginary friend, I was, as far as I could tell, deeply in love with Jeannie, and I think I understand now why she felt compelled to create the curious character I found on the edge of the bed that night. I believe Jeannie was terribly insecure, afraid that she, by herself, just wasn't sexy enough to satisfy me. Of course she was very wrong, and I must have sensed some of that even then, because I assured her repeatedly that although I quite enjoyed Betty Sue's company, I preferred Jeannie in every way I could imagine. I swore that she was all I'd ever wanted, all I would ever need, and I meant it. After our wonderful week together in Hyannisport, Jeannie and Betty Sue went back to Cincinnati on a single ticket, and the band moved on. But the two of us remained madly, profoundly, desperately in love, and I believed, or hoped, that this romance, unlike all those before it, might actually endure. Okay, so I'm a little slow on the uptake.

From Cape Cod *Sunrise* traveled to New Hampshire or Buffalo or Somerville, or maybe it was Rhode Island, and through it all Jeannie and I hung on, writing and calling despite the now routine (to me) impossibility of our relationship. To the best of my recollection, I was almost faithful to her for an impressive period of time. And soon *Sunrise* headed west again toward Colorado to take a little time off and regroup.

On the way back to Denver I stopped in Ohio, where I spent a few days with Jeannie before continuing west. But although we were still passionate and in love, it was becoming apparent that she was not happy, that our distance was taking its toll, as it inevitably did. Still, it wasn't until the final day of my visit that Jeannie actually broached the subject of her dissatisfaction. She needed someone who was present, she explained through her sobs, someone she could see and touch every day. And I suppose I was just a chicken shit; I didn't say, "Okay, I'll move to Cincinnati and get a real job," or "Come with me and we will find a way to make it work." I was still unwilling to take that chance, and it was probably very sad. I was probably very sad.

I was still immersed in the fresh pain of losing Jeannie when yet another personal tragedy arose. Following our brief hiatus in Denver, the band had traveled south to Colorado Springs, where we were booked at a club about which I remember nothing at all when the telephone wakened me early one morning. It was my mother calling to inform me that my grandmother was dead. I thanked her for the call and went back to my bed, where I quietly wept for what might have been hours.

My grandmother had been a parent to me, and she had died while I was away, unable to comfort her at the end, or to somehow stop the end from coming. I didn't have the opportunity to say goodbye or to tell her again that I loved her; I didn't get to hear her tell me one more time how handsome or sweet I was, and I felt wretched. I had, in the end, been unable to protect either one of us.

I remember silently dedicating a song to Anna that night, and I remember still the tears streaming down my swollen red cheeks as I tried to sing. Even now, when I allow myself to think of her, I miss her terribly. And then I smile a little.

17

Gorilla Warfare

At some point in the midst of my confusion and pain, our management agency decided that the band was too large to be financially viable—the economy was changing and clubs were hiring DJs at a fraction of the cost of a medium-sized band. So without fanfare, and with very little deliberation, we discarded Kathy, Nancy, Bill and Phil, the nice but unremarkable baritone player and singer we had hired just a couple months earlier in Ohio. The newly formed band's first booking was in a cozy Denver club called Carboni's, where I slept with a cute little waitress, and where I very nearly got myself murdered.

During a break one night I observed Melanie, the waitress I would soon be corrupting, struggling to make her way around the large body that was eclipsing the entrance to the service bar. When the ungainly thug didn't seem to notice, or to care, I approached him from behind. I reached up to tap his massive shoulder, and requested, in the friendliest, most respectful tone possible, that he step aside and let her do her job. He swung around, creating a warm gust, and glowered down at me before lifting me up by my armpits and tossing me across the room like a poorly dressed puppet. I think what he mumbled as I whizzed through the air was, "Duh, how would you like it if I pushed *you?*"

After my landing, for some reason I can't now even imagine, I marched back toward him, beer bottle still in hand, and said, "I think you just did." It was then that his two gargantuan friends suddenly appeared. One of them just leered down at me while the other one suggested in unequivocal grunts that it wasn't a very good idea to "tret'n" Vinnie. But unaware that the bottle I was gripping was now broken and could quite reasonably be perceived as a potential weapon, I continued foolishly explaining to the three primates that I felt maybe Vinnie had overreacted just a teensy weensy bit. As they moved ominously closer, confirming their evil intentions, I stepped back, set the bottle down, and, fearing certain death, did the only thing I could think of. That's right, I grabbed a huge chair, raised it over my head, and warned with impressive mock-bravery, "I know I'm going to die, but before I do, at least one of you is going to sustain a serious head injury, which, I admit, may or may not have any obvious effect, but which will, nevertheless, smart like the dickens." To my astonishment, they retreated (possibly out of boredom), and I put the chair down and strode quietly, nervously back toward the stage.

The first song of the next set was *Car Wash*, which I always began by clicking my drumsticks together rhythmically for eight bars or so before the rest of the band joined in, clapping hands to the same insipid rhythm. But this time, at about the fifth or sixth bar, I felt the sticks slip from my hands. When I looked up, the big panting goon from the bar was gripping them in his massive claws and threatening to "Fuck me up." First I swung my expensive microphone out of harm's way, and then, to my astonishment, I picked up the cymbal stand with which I apparently hoped to defend myself. When the monstrosity tore the steel stand from me and split it easily in two, John leapt out from behind the light board and onto his back. Suddenly, the two auxiliary gorillas jumped on John, pulling him and his grunting prey over a railing and on to the carpet. Aware now that I might have to die in an effort to aid my friend and brave defender, I flew out from behind my drums. Suddenly I was face to face with the menacing beast, who was shaking what remained of John off of his powerful simian shoulders. He scowled and snarled. And then something very odd happened. Just as I was giving serious consideration to sincere, heartfelt prayer, the three apes rushed across the room on their hairy knuckles and hustled out the door.

The first order of business, upon my return to civilized society and a near normal heart-rate, was to care for John, who was trying to get a look at the gaping wound that had formed across his back. He was in some pain and his shirt was torn and bloody, but it seemed he would survive without lengthy hospitalization. As we were trying to reassemble the stage and our equipment, I began to wonder again why they'd left so quickly, and without at least one or two of my vital organs. I knew I couldn't have scared them when I came out to face them; any one of them could have squashed my skull with one paw while picking a gaggle of mites off his own matted fur with the other. It made no sense until the end of the night—which could not have come too soon—when one of the beta males returned and began examining the floor in front of the stage. Without a word, he diligently combed the entire area until he finally pulled something dark and hairy from the carpet by the stage and casually lumbered out.

What we later learned was that when John attacked the alpha, he apparently unseated the toupee' that had, until then, been a well-kept, shameful secret. Kong had run out in bald embarrassment. I guess it isn't true that humans are the only animals who blush. My life was saved by a hairpiece.

And...

Before we left that night, the uniformed officer, who had calmly observed the entire episode from the comfort of the bar, approached me and said, "I'm awfully sorry, but I don't fuck with those mob guys. The big one is a boxer, and they all carry guns." We apprehensively finished our brief engagement at Carboni's before heading south to the theoretical safety of Alamogordo, New Mexico.

18

Tremors

Alamogordo, the small dusty city in South-Central New Mexico where the first atomic bomb was exploded on Monday, July 16, 1945, was, and presumably still is, primarily a military town, mostly run and often overrun by the proud men and women of the United States Air Force. Contrary to what we'd feared, they were a particularly friendly and appreciative audience.

One night, early in our visit to the well-protected town, Ed and I somehow befriended two fetching women. There was Betty, who for some reason she never explained, preferred to be called Chuck, and Tara, who seemed perfectly satisfied with the name she'd been assigned. As we headed home after an enjoyable late-night breakfast with these lovely and unexpectedly interesting women, Ed confided to me with an uneasy combination of enthusiasm and dread that he had never been as attracted to anyone as he was to Tara. He appealed to me, as Bill had concerning Nancy, to respect his potential developing romance. Tara oozed sexuality and was vibrant and entertaining, but I had a feeling that it might prove a wise choice to honor Ed's request, even if I didn't like him. And I should say, at this point, that although I never really believed I had the power over women that my friends and coworkers attributed to me, it was nice to have their respect and admiration.

So while I was getting acquainted with Betty, whom I soon learned was a sweet, sensitive, and very bright but unhappy young Air Force wife, Ed was, to everyone's surprise and concern, having great success with Tara, who was also an unhappy young Air Force wife. While

Betty and I took our time, kissing for hours, making out with most of our clothing on, and occasionally slipping a timid hand in to touch moist eager flesh—acting the way teenagers theoretically did in those distant days—Ed was in body-fluid heaven with Tara. We were a happy, if amoral, bunch.

But one evening as I was strolling from the stage toward the table where Tara and Betty were waiting, I noticed a particularly sexy young woman with a beautifully sculpted face, fine and notable breasts, and long, slender, delicious legs, sitting with a wide and very muscular man who had a head the size and shape of a large American station wagon, possibly an Oldsmobile. When I smiled in their direction—my general, all-purpose, golly-gee friendly guy smile, rather than my specific, flirtatious, please get rid of the big bozo and fuck me smile—they both smiled back. A second later the woman stood up and intercepted me. After telling me how much she and her "friend" enjoyed the band, she asked if I'd like to join them for a drink, and following informal introductions I sat down at their table. Jeannie (that's right) and I conversed and flirted while Jim attempted to draw the attention of a waitress in order to order the drink they'd offered. Finally, impatient and visibly frustrated, Jim stomped toward the bar. By the time he returned, Jeannie (who would never know if I called her by my ex-girlfriend's name) had agreed to visit me the following night, without her bodyguard.

I'd become quite fond of Betty, but she was married. But probably more to the point, Jeannie was one of those women whom you simply must, if offered the opportunity, see naked. And anyway, I was completely out of control. As advertised, Jeannie showed up alone the next night, looking even more appetizing than she had the night before. And Betty, hurt but outwardly more understanding than I could have dared to expect—undoubtedly more understanding than I deserved—left early.

Born and raised in Las Vegas and employed in Alamogordo as a legal secretary, Jeannie was unenthusiastically involved in a passionless relationship with Jim, the massive Air Force pilot she'd been sitting with the night I met her. She knew little about her main father, she explained, but her mother had, in the years following his final disappearance, been involved with or married to a series of violent alcoholics generally known to Jeannie as "Uncle Next." She'd witnessed hostility and bloodshed for most of her life, and she suffered too from hypoglycemia, an illness about which, at that point, I knew nothing.

After much wine and lovemaking in Jeannie's mobile home that night, we finally fell asleep, but at around six o'clock in the morning the trailer shook even more intensely than it had hours earlier. "Earthquake?" I asked when I saw that she too had been awakened by the violent rumbling.

Her lovely pale-green eyes glowed with dread as she leapt, naked, from the bed. "Jim," she responded with suitable terror.

"Where's the back door?"

She battled an obstinate nightgown, her entire body quivering. "There isn't one," she groaned.

"Where would you like it?"

I shot out of bed and dressed faster than I ever had before or would again and made my way to the living room couch, where I sat, trying to look innocent and relaxed as Jeannie unlocked the now buckling door to admit the irate Air Force pilot.

"What the fuck is going on here?" the dinosauric aberration screamed, in full uniform, and clearly agitated.

"You are fucking dead." He held out a fist the size and shape of a canned ham. "And you, you god-damned whore."

I was convinced we were both about to die, and I searched my reeling mind for a way out while Jeannie stood behind him, pale and as silent as a stone. As he leveled his rage first at me and then at her, Jim's agitation seemed to increase. I was waiting for my short life to flash in front of me, hoping it would be a little better this time, when a desperate idea began to take hazy form.

"Jim," I finally interrupted, feeling stark terror, but feigning anger. "If you would just *shut up* long enough to listen, you'd realize what a complete *ass* you're making of yourself."

Like a stunned deer caught in the headlights of an oncoming truck, he stopped dead in his tracks. Nervously, I continued my still developing tirade. "Jesus Christ," I said with counterfeit disgust, "you should be ashamed of yourself."

Jeannie was still standing silently behind him, as confused as he was and turning almost transparent with terror.

"What the fuck are you talking about, slick?" he finally said.

"You've got this wonderful woman," I continued, "but you're *so* ready to assume the worst. You know, you really don't de*serve* her." It was obvious that the force and the simple fact of my assault had momentarily caught the lumbering hulk off guard. What kind of idiot would be dumb enough to scream at you and call you names after getting caught fucking your girlfriend? "Well," I said, trying to look offended, my own blood and bile backing up in my throat like a low flow toilet, "if you want to believe that *this* woman," gesturing toward her, "who obviously loves you *very* much, was unfaithful, you go right ahead. But if you give a shit about her, you might want to listen to what *really* happened."

Jim wanted to murder me, I'm certain, and at least dismember Jeannie. His tiny little brain was screaming, "Kill, kill, kill," but there was another almost human voice saying, "Okay, hold on now. Whoa, horsy."

"All right, slick," he responded with grim sarcasm. "What's *your* story?"

I still had no idea what I was going to say when I began. "As you know Jim, I am playing in the band at…"

"No shit." He interrupted violently.

"Well, the band, Jim," I pronounced his name with caustic precision, "is sharing a small house, two to a room, which would normally be fine, but which became a problem when Sarah, our guitar player's brand new wife, came down from Denver to pay him a surprise visit on his birthday." His birthday! If I lived I would be proud. "They hadn't seen each other in months and all they wanted was to be alone for *one* night. When Jeannie overheard us discussing the difficulty of sleeping arrangements, *Jim*, she was thoughtful enough to offer me the comfort of her couch." Like a good attorney, I was mounting an assault, using a barrage of not entirely credible lies to create just the slightest hint of doubt, aware that the prosecution had no *hard* proof.

The Air Force pilot just glared at me, flustered and uncertain, veins slowly receding on his spacious rectangular forehead as the first hints of color began to reappear, along with an expression of respectful incredulity, on Jeannie's stunning, angular face.

"Look Jim," I said more calmly. "I don't care about myself, but you definitely owe Jeannie an apology. She is a *very* special woman," somber smile, "and you are damned lucky to have her, if you haven't already fucked it up with this furious display."

Jim stood there for another minute before turning to look at Jeannie and then back toward me. "Okay Slick," he said, his voice and body shaking as though there were a fierce fistfight raging inside him, "I'm going to let you go for now, because there's a tiny chance that you're telling the truth, but I'm telling you, and I want you to hear me," he grew louder, "that I don't *ever* want you coming around here again. Now get the hell out of here before I *really* lose my temper, you fucking little asshole." I shot past him, squinting in anticipation of a deadly blow to the back of my head, and slid through the doorway. "You never talk to her or call her on the phone or even think about her or I swear to God, I'll fucking kill you, you son-of-a-bitch," he ordered as I stepped into my trusty red Datsun. It wasn't until I got back to the house where we were staying that I noticed I wasn't wearing my socks. In my panic I had left them on the floor next to Jeannie's bed.

Later that afternoon, when despite Jim's admonition I phoned Jeannie at her office, she reported that only ten minutes after my hasty departure, Jim had discovered my telltale footwear and become enraged for a second time. She'd quickly invented an implausible story involving a severe backache and a brief, innocent, fully-clothed back-rub. But although he didn't quite believe her, he still had no real proof of what had happened. Jim finally decided to let her live, while vowing that if he ever saw me again he would shoot me in the face. Jeannie was physically uninjured, but terribly upset.

It wasn't until the following day, when I received reports from various sources, including Jeannie, that Jim was driving one of his two Corvettes around town with a loaded shotgun perched upright in the passenger's seat, that I finally recognized the gravity of the situation. Duh. In terrified desperation, I called him at home and told him that if he didn't stay away from me I would report him to his commanding officer and the military and local police and even his mother if he had one. If he wasn't arrested, I warned, he would certainly be grounded (by the air force, not his mother), which would cost him his considerable flight pay. All he said before slamming the phone down was, "Fuck you." It seemed apparent that I just couldn't do *anything* to satisfy him.

But...

Despite the threat to my life, I continued to spend time with Jeannie. And Jim, of course, soon found out. Even Betty, who was still in the picture, though sadly fading fast (and whom I still regret having hurt, if, in fact, I did) was concerned for my safety. This was not good. This was bad.

And...

On our final ominous day in the little military town I witnessed an unforgettable act of nature, an act of nature that at the time seemed curiously fitting. It was my first and only dust storm, and I was duly impressed.

What began as a temperamental morning breeze, sending stinging swarms of sand whipping through the air, became within an hour a wildly bellowing wind, racing unobstructed across endless miles of warm, arid desert. And as the wind grew, the sky slowly darkened, turning a deep, rich amber before becoming the palpable, heavy, gray-brown substance that filled my burning eyes and tasted like antediluvian dirt. For an hour or so it was as dark as a moonlit night, and hours later, after the brutal winds had finally relented, the rain began. Not a clean refreshing rain, but a thick, dark, disgusting brown rain; it was mudding. How strange.

We played and sang and coughed dryly that last dust and mud covered night, nervously anticipating our bloody demise while our military and civilian friends in the audience, many of whom had followed our troublesome exploits, sat at the tables and chairs they'd lined up in front of the stage, fully prepared, they said, to stand and face whatever assault might be waged upon us. I guess Jim didn't have a lot of friends in the Air Force. Fortunately, and remarkably, the long night passed without bloodshed. Having destroyed or damaged an impressive percentage of the marriages and intimate relationships in Alamogordo, we left town early the following morning, both Tara and Jeannie following just weeks behind. And several angry armed soldiers following just days behind them.

In spite of Jim's frightening, unanticipated late night visit the following week to the hotel where we were staying, and in spite of the less than luxurious living arrangements in which we found ourselves, Jeannie and I did all right for a time. But she was seeking the glamour that seldom really exists in the life of a working musician, and a secure home and future—things I was uniquely ill-prepared to offer.

Night after night I watched while she suffered the tormenting effects of her body's chemical imbalance, learning more about who Jeannie really was, and maybe a little more about myself. Often I would kneel on the floor beside the bed and massage her "buzzing" legs as she tried, and frequently failed, to sleep. Then, in the morning, her blood sugar fluctuating wildly, she would snarl and moan and complain nastily about nothing until she'd ravened a perfectly balanced breakfast. Nevertheless, we had fun for a while, and I suppose we both did what we could to make it work, but life with me wasn't what she had hoped it might be.

And yet, though I had sensed that something else was wrong, I had no idea what was really missing from my crumbling relationship with Jeannie until, months later in Wichita, Kansas, I met Nancy. Nancy, who would steal my faithless heart.

19

The End of an Error

Nancy, a subtly stunning, petite brunette who was waiting tables at the club where we were playing in Wichita, was by far the most appealing component of a large group of people with whom I went out to breakfast one night after work. I had noticed her, of course, and flirted timidly with her a few times, and I remember talking with her for no particular reason about children and the cruelty they sometimes endured at the hands of their caretakers. But I really knew nothing about her except that she was truly lovely, that she seemed very sweet, and that she shared my sentiments about the mistreatment of children.

Nancy and I found ourselves sitting next to each other in the restaurant that night, and before long we were holding hands under the table. Two nights later, after coercing Ed to spend the night in my car (I had once done the same for him), I invited Nancy back to the hotel. And in the morning when we awoke to the sound of the hotel maid's timid knocking, Nancy and I were enveloped in a twisted cocoon of moist, fragrant sheets and blankets, holding each other close, arms and legs intertwined. "Would you like me to make up your room today," the maid asked through the double-locked door. "No thanks," I said as I'd done so many times in so many hotels before, "but we could use more towels."

Nancy was gentle and affectionate; she possessed a tenderness that Jeannie had lacked and that I'd apparently been missing without ever realizing it. And though I know how weary you must be of hearing this, how shopworn the phrase must sound, how impossible it must be to believe, it didn't take us very long to fall in love. I suppose Jeannie had simply become the woman she'd had to be to exist and survive in her peculiar, perilous world, while Nancy had evolved in a different way through her own painful life. But what they, and most of the sad, unfortunate women with whom I had and would continue to become involved, had in common, was the history of grief that seemed to attract me with such destructive force. Still, Nancy was warmer and more accessible than Jeannie had ever been. She allowed herself to be vulnerable and she expressed her love in ways that I could understand, ways that I could feel. I could hold and comfort her without the fear of a surprise attack, and she could hold and comfort me—something I so desperately needed. I, of course, had been damaged too. Poor Nancy; poor me.

In the few weeks we spent together in Wichita, Nancy and I incited the fiery beginning of a profound and passionate love, but once again time was limited. As always, the band would soon be moving on. Nevertheless, by the time I had to depart for El Paso, Nancy and I were cautiously but enthusiastically discussing, and actually beginning to believe in, our eternal blissful future together. Isn't it amazing how desperately we need to believe?

In El Paso, just an hour or so south of Alamogordo, our band and everyone in it went by assumed names, just to be safe from the well-armed military husbands still encamped on the Holloman Air Force base, only a couple hours to the north. Terrified, but desperate to believe in her and in us, I called and wrote to Nancy every day. I had learned by then that even the most warm and compelling feelings could be suddenly, unexpectedly destroyed. Or maybe that was merely an excuse, a justification for the gratifying but passionless blowjob to which I submitted late one night in my car on a mountain road overlooking the oil-stained border town.

From dingy, arid El Paso, we traveled through almost unbearable heat to Lawton, Oklahoma, another mostly military town, where I found that I missed Nancy so much that I was unable to focus on anything else. Of course there was little else to do in Lawton, outside of watching the incessant tornado warnings and watches on the television in our stuffy rooms. But it became apparent, during our many long telephone conversations those first days in Lawton, that something was wrong. What a fucking surprise.

What I learned when she flew down to see me the following week was that while I was feeling so sorry for myself because I had to endure the arduous drive from El Paso to Lawton without air-conditioning in one-hundred and ten degree heat, Nancy was undergoing an abortion. She had been pregnant when I met her, she sheepishly explained in my dark, impersonal motel room, and had made the difficult decision to end her pregnancy without the help or support of the man whose developing child she was relinquishing. Steve, the manager at the club where Nancy and I had met, and where they both continued to work, wanted nothing whatsoever to do with her or with the unintended product of their intimacy—the worthless fuck.

Understandably, Nancy had been afraid to tell me; she'd feared that I would be angry or hurt, or that I might judge her harshly. She'd been afraid too—and I still think this is so terribly sad—that I would be upset because we couldn't make love while she her body recuperated from the operation. Through all of this I did the best I could to understand and to lovingly comfort and care for Nancy, and we became even closer through the sharing of her anguish. When I really wanted to, and when I allowed myself to, I could be decent and caring, and it felt surprisingly good.

As she began to feel safer and more comfortable in our relationship, Nancy shared with me, in bleak bits and pieces, her history of loss and abuse. Her life, she explained, had been threatened repeatedly by her mentally disordered mother, who would stand silently over her bed, clutching a butcher knife as Nancy squinted up, horrified, through the early morning darkness. And her older brother, just a year before Nancy and I met, had hanged himself from a tree in the woods near their home in Syracuse, New York. And of course there was more drama, more trauma. There always is.

But Nancy had ultimately escaped, physically at least, leaving Syracuse with a young man who soon abandoned her for another woman. Since then she'd been supporting herself, living alone, and trying to make sense of her life. Although I knew nothing of her history when we met, I feel certain now that I somehow sensed her grief and suffering from the very beginning, and that it was at least a part of the intangible force that drew me so forcefully toward her. I recognized it; it was frighteningly familiar to me. I was home.

It's strange how we always seem to recreate our histories, vainly attempting to do better this time, to correct our earlier mistakes and fulfill the many remaining unfulfilled needs. I'm not certain we have any choice, but sadly, very sadly I think, it doesn't work. Inevitably we do the same things in the same ways, repeating the worst of our fleeting lives. We do what we know. Lucky us.

After leaving Oklahoma *Sunrise* headed back to Denver, where, weeks later, Nancy paid me another sweet and wonderful visit. It was around nine o'clock in the morning when she knocked on the door of the apartment where Ron and I were encamped. But the day after her unexpected arrival, Ron, in a drunken stupor, set the place on fire. Nancy and I were forced to move into the motel where I'd been living months before with Jeannie. And I admit, with apposite shame, the sense of pride I felt, checking in again, just months later, with yet another gorgeous woman in tow.

Nancy stayed with me for a week before going back to work, and *Sunrise* continued to perform in and around Denver. But Nancy and I were no longer willing to continue living apart, and soon we began to plan my escape to Wichita, which, as I think of it now, seems a peculiar concept. Isn't Wichita the sort of place *from* which one escapes?

And then I suffered another painful loss. In Golden, Colorado, after years of good and faithful service, with almost two hundred thousand miles on the odometer, my ailing Datsun finally, tragically died. As far as I know, Herman still sits rusting and telling incredible tales of beautiful women, love, and sex to the skeptical Audis, Volvos, and BMWs parked around him in the gravel parking lot behind the building where our management company then had its offices. And so, without a car, and with no clear (or vague) plan for financial survival, I finally presented the band with my formal resignation.

But...

We had all worked together for a long time; we had learned to truly like and respect one another. Despite my eagerness to make a home with Nancy and to try to restructure my life, I regretted having to relinquish my friends. Therefore, I agreed to remain for the duration of the existing bookings, at which time, everyone agreed, the entire band would disband. Fittingly, I guess, the last three weeks of *Sunrise's* final month together were spent back in Wichita.

Just a month or so earlier, John, our guitarist, had quit the band in order to spend more time with his new wife. After a series of disappointing auditions, we had, in desperation, hired a competent but angry fellow whose name I have chosen to forget. For weeks we'd tolerated his unpleasant nature and increasingly hostile temper, but in Wichita I decided, after another of his offensive outbursts, to fire him. I said simply, "Go home."

"What do you mean," he asked, apparently bewildered.

"You're fired. You are an asshole, and I refuse to spend my final weeks with this band putting up with your ridiculous, infantile bullshit."

"You can't fire me without notice...in Kansas."

"You're probably right, but I just did. You don't have to go home if you don't want to, just go away."

And sweet John, who was still living in Denver with his wife, flew out the following morning to work the remaining nights with us. He didn't do it for the money; he did it for us, and for the fun of it. And we *did* have fun; Ron even sobered up for our final night in order to watch the rest of us get profoundly drunk. For all I know, the ugly experience may have cured him. These were good, honorable, and relatively talented people and I would miss them. I did miss them.

So...

It was in this way that, suddenly, at the age of twenty-three, I found myself living in Wichita, Kansas, without a job, a plan, a marketable skill, without even a means of transportation. But I had Nancy, our shared love, and her amazing, passionate, high-powered, soaking wet multiple orgasms. Who needed a car? Oh yeah, and Nancy bought me a Mazda pickup truck with custom wheels, a fiberglass cap, and glass packs. And we were happy...for a time.

20

Storms

I can still remember as I write this now, how exquisitely beautiful Nancy was, and how much I cherished her. But I can also feel the rage and pain I felt when she finally, brutally decimated my heart.

As I look back through the sometimes welcome and forgiving filter of twenty-two years of frantic, desperate living, I realize that I was disintegrating, coming apart emotionally. Maybe it was the abrupt end, after so many years of aimless, frenzied motion; perhaps when I finally put on the brakes, all that I'd left behind continued careening forward at the speed of noise, striking me in the back of the head like a truckload of lumber. Involved for the first time in a truly committed adult relationship, maybe I was just terribly vulnerable, and scared to death.

But I tried; *we* tried.

I searched for work, first as a musician, and then, when I couldn't find a decent local band that wanted or needed my alleged skills, I began warily perusing the want ads for a *real* job. Nancy was patient and understanding, supporting us both on her meager salary and inconstant tips without complaint, while I unenthusiastically investigated other employment options. For a few weeks I actually worked in a bar, serving beer, adopting a pathetically sad and confused expression when anything more complex was ordered. "Could somebody please tell me what goes into a gin and tonic?" Through all the vicissitudes, Nancy and I tried to make a home and a life together, and we were, for a time, sweet and loving to one another. I still believe that we loved one another dearly. And there were some beautiful moments that I will never forget.

Sometimes, late at night, we would sit gazing out the wide picture window, holding each other close, watching the brilliant summer storms as they flashed and thundered in their deliberate approach from the inky blackness in the west, bringing with them translucent silver sheets of windswept rain. We made love with a perfect combination of tenderness and passion. We played and laughed hard and sometimes cried harder. And the storms kept coming.

The fact is, and it amazes me as much as anyone, that, in spite of the very puissant temptation of Wichita's other available prey, I'd remained faithful to Nancy since the minor blowjob I received in El Paso. Although there was one very close call.

I first encountered Mary during my search for work as a drummer in a club where a popular local band was playing. She was very sexy, well-assembled, unhappily married, outgoing, and apparently interested in me. We exchanged numbers that night, and within a week we got as far as sharing a bottle of wine alone in her apartment. But when it came time to act, I couldn't even bring myself to kiss her. Awkwardly, I apologized for my reluctance to be unfaithful, assuring her that under any other circumstances, I would not have been able to control myself around her—and it was true, of course. She confessed that she was disappointed, but as I was leaving she purred, "Oh well, at least I have my vibrator." With that arousing image blazing in my sick little mind, I nearly turned around.

But I had unknowingly relinquished what little identity I'd possessed. I was no longer a drummer, a singer, a comedian, or a lecher; I was lost and confused and, I guess, scared to death by what I felt when the distraction of the noise and commotion suddenly ceased. So when my brother Scott called several months after my arrival in Kansas and asked me to come to New York to record some of his music with him, I decided, after a truly agonizing internal debate, that I should go. I wasn't abandoning Nancy, I told myself; I was simply making an effort to somehow recapture what I felt I'd lost, and hoping that she would soon follow. So I packed my drums and some of my clothing into the noisy little truck Nancy had bought me, and headed toward New York City, leaving her behind, probably at least as frightened and confused as I was.

Leaving Nancy was a mistake, of course—not that staying would have worked out any better. And although Scott and I did eventually do some sporadic recording in New York, it was a long and tedious process that would, in the end, come to little more than an educational experience in terms of my floundering musical career.

For several lonely months I slept on the couch in Scott's small studio apartment, while he slept, or didn't, on his twin bed just a couple of feet away. Scott's congenial cat, Al, was able to leap from great heights and land solidly on all four painfully pointy paws with an impressive thud; he would regularly prove it shortly after I'd finally fallen asleep, using my torso as a landing pad. He was otherwise a fine and loving companion.

But sharing a tiny apartment in Queens with my older brother was not an effortless undertaking. I'm sure it was difficult for him too—probably more so—but he was extremely good to me nonetheless, and we got along surprisingly well. Though Scott and I have always had an imperfect relationship, as I suppose brothers often do, we were able to live and work together for months. Meanwhile, Nancy and I struggled to keep our faltering, long-distance love alive, writing and phoning and crying and worrying as the emotional chasm that had developed between us gradually broadened.

It was while I was staying with Scott that Nancy learned of her sister's terminal cancer, and it was then that I became deeply concerned for her and for us. Even before that grim occurrence, there had been some subtle but undeniable hints of the dangers to which I had, by that time, become so sensitive. I'd felt her drifting away from me, I thought, and perhaps toward someone else. But now, I believed, I hoped, she needed me. So at about four o'clock one morning, after a long night of drinking and a brief detour to Kennedy airport, where I left my younger brother, Christopher, waiting for his flight to Germany, I began the long trek back to Kansas. And outside of the essential interruptions for gas and food, I stopped only once, in Cincinnati, where I tried to sleep for an hour or so on Jeannie's living room couch. Though I did not pursue it, and most likely would not have been successful if I had, to deny that I thought about sleeping *with* her would be dishonest. And we wouldn't want that.

Jeannie was kind, understanding, and generous. And as she was leaving for work shortly after my unheralded arrival early that afternoon, she told me she had a couple hundred dollars in her dresser drawer, and that I should take whatever I needed. I borrowed a hundred. It was countless long, sleepless hours later, when, looking nearly as dreadful as I felt, I walked in on Nancy.

She didn't know I was coming; *I* didn't know I was coming, but there I stood, unshaven and trembling in her doorway, anxiously hoping she would welcome me home. I doubt I would have survived for so long without sleep if it hadn't been for my insane jealousy and my sincere but almost psychotic concern for Nancy's well-being. It's amazing what one can do with a little psychopathic energy. And I'm honestly not certain which of those forces was more compelling. I'd like to believe that my desire to care for her was more powerful than my fears of losing her, but I just don't know. I only know that I felt a great number of compelling, sometimes conflicting emotions, and that I did what I did.

And I was right to be concerned. Nancy had been sharing her sadness, if nothing else, with the evil Jerry Argutin, an insurance salestwit© she'd met at the bar. He was just watching and waiting for an opportunity to pounce, for her to have a moment of weakness. I hated him with a deadly passion. I suppose I still do.

Yes, I do.

While Jerry lurked in the bushes or under a moist rock, and Nancy's sister's hopeless condition continued to deteriorate, Nancy and I struggled to reclaim our damaged love. But there was disquieting evidence of my increasing emotional frailty when, despite Nancy's vulnerability,

I vented my rage on a carload of drunken strangers who had carelessly or intentionally run us off the road late one night, my violent explosion terrifying both Nancy and myself as I forced them into the roadside brush at seventy-five miles-an-hour.

And it wasn't long after that incident that Nancy found the letter from Jeannie that, believing I had nothing to hide, I'd left out.

"I got your message," she snapped when I dropped her off at work that evening.

"What message," I asked, completely baffled as she shoved the door open.

"The letter from your *friend*, Jeannie, that you left out for me to see." She slammed the door and disappeared through the bar's entrance.

While Nancy was at work that evening, I remained at home. I grew more and more livid as I repeatedly, obsessively visualized the altercation that would follow her return. I allowed myself a succession of increasingly violent fantasies, fantasies wherein I stomped around the cluttered apartment explaining in progressively louder and angrier tones that the letter I'd left out had no more meaning than the camera or the tape recorder I hadn't put away for weeks. In my scalded mind I watched myself screaming and kicking the various proofs of my careless but innocent behavior. Finally, when I thought I'd exhausted my rage, I took a breath and sat down. The ugly scene I was anticipating would only be counterproductive, I resolved. What was really needed was a calm, logical, loving discussion. I decided I would pick her up at work and drive her home, where I would request a quiet moment to explain the silly misunderstanding in which we'd somehow allowed ourselves to become embroiled. Everything would be okay.

We drove home in tense, deadly silence that night, and when we were inside I asked Nancy to sit on the couch across from me so we could talk about what she had said, and how much it had hurt me. I swallowed, fighting my searing wrath as I began. "I've had a lot of time to think about what you said when you left the truck this evening." I felt and heard my heart pounding, but knew I must remain relaxed and in control. Then, I reached mechanically over to the end table on my right, lifted it off the floor, and heaved it across the room, shattering the glass picture window through which we'd watched so many storms. I was bellowing epithets I don't care to recall. I was completely out of control, and it horrified us both. When the storm was over, I sat trembling and weeping, finally melting shamefully into the chair where I was going to calmly explain how much she had hurt me.

Several bleak and cheerless days later, Nancy's sister went into a coma, and by the time Nancy's plane landed in Syracuse, her sister had succumbed. Nancy never had the opportunity to say goodbye.

On the telephone from Syracuse, Nancy, sobbing between every word, told me how she screamed and ran to stop them when they began to lower the coffin into the ground. I was not there of course, but the awful image is permanently imbedded in my mind.

It is raining lightly. A beautiful girl stands by a shallow rectangular cavity in the moist cemetery ground. She is crying, strands of long dark hair slapping lightly at her grief-swollen face as she pleads with her family, with friends, and strangers not to bury her poor dead sister. Finally, something in her shatters. She mouths a silent goodbye to a cold emaciated corpse encased in a sinking wooden box.

If I'd had any money of my own, and if she'd wanted me to, I would have gone with her, not that it would have made any real difference. At least that is what I tell myself now. But as it was, all I could do was wait for her tearful return, and then try very hard to put my own needs and insecurities aside for a while. At least that is what I tell myself now.

I'm not sure when it really ended, if it was when I first left for New York, or after I returned. I don't know if there was still a chance for us after my first savage outburst, but by the time Nancy returned from Syracuse, all that remained was a vague sweet memory mostly obscured by a cold, impenetrable wall of anger and wrenching sorrow. And Jerry was still waiting, slithering.

Still, for a time Nancy and I continued to go through the motions, still needing each other's love and support, but terrified of getting close again. And occasionally we made love. We struggled with each other and ourselves, reaching out tentatively and then retreating at the first hint of danger, real or imagined.

And Jerry was a patient weasel. The night I finally met him, he was having drinks with a friend at one of Nancy's tables. I was relaxing at the bar with my friend Mike Elliot, a part-time bartender at the club, waiting for Nancy to finish work, when she offered to introduce me to the scumbucket I'd already heard more than enough about. With great reluctance, I strode over to his table, drink in hand, and after awkward introductions, I coolly accepted Jerry's offer to join them. I hated this guy already, and there was nothing in the world he could have said or done to alter that, but what he and his friend did, was make that pungent, but strangely satisfying feeling even stronger.

"So Grant, I understand you live in New York."

"No, Jerry. I live here, with Nancy."

"Oh, I thought you were just visiting."

"No. I live here."

"Well, haven't you been living in New York?"

"No, I've been *visit*ing New York. I live with Nancy." I smiled widely, viciously.

"But you are going back to New York, right? And aren't you from there?"

"I'm from Pennsylvania."

"Uh huh."

"But *now* I live with Nancy."

"So, what are your plans, Grant?"

"My plans, Jerry?"

"Well, are you going back home?"

"Home?" The tension was building and my heart was racing.

"Yeah, back east. That's still home right? I mean that's where you're from."

"What do you want to know, Jerry? Do you want to know where I'm from or where I live or what? I don't understand the question. What would you like to know?" Nancy walked by and sensed the friction.

"Well..." he began.

I interrupted him. "I was born in Allentown, Pennsylvania. When I was seven or eight years old we moved to Emmaus; that's right outside of Allentown. Then, when my mother was offered a better job, we moved to the Pocono Mountains, where we lived first in a large home along the lush green banks of the Delaware River, and then in a series of other homes scattered through the bucolic Pennsylvania countryside. We continued moving around, Jerry—and please let me know if I'm going too fast for you 'cause you don't seem so smart—until I left home and began to work as a musician, traveling all over the United States and Canada until finally meeting Nancy, you know, your waitress, with whom I now live and where, you stupid fuck, I plan to remain."

I turned to Jerry's perplexed and perspiring friend and said, "I don't know you, but your pal, Jerry, is a fucking asshole. It really doesn't reflect well on you." Suddenly, my friend Mike was standing at my side, asking me with gentle firmness to sit with him and his younger brother, Mark. I smiled and complied. And within thirty minutes Jerry was surrounded by six or so big, doofy, gym class dropouts who had apparently been summoned to protect him or to threaten me, I'm still not sure which.

Mike and his brother were sweet. They recognized the potential for a one-sided blood bath in which I would be violently eviscerated, and they did everything they could to calm me and draw my attention away from the table of idiot insurance agents, or whatever the fuck they were. Unfortunately, my anger was not to be controlled; the more I thought about Jerry and his cellmates, the more irate I became. Finally, when someone at the other table made a loud, inarticulate, and less than complimentary reference to me, I exploded. "Fuck you," I screamed, standing up with my belt wrapped around my fist. "You stupid fucking assholes." I too, could have done better.

Amazingly, nothing happened. Of course Nancy couldn't have been more upset. Under the circumstances, my behavior was unforgivable. But there was no physical contact between the two factions—no carnage. The only response from Jerry came later that night in the form of a large footprint in the door of the pickup truck Nancy had bought me—pretty lame. I (well, Nancy) was well insured.

Before I finally left Kansas and Nancy for the last time, things got a little better, and then they got worse again. Jerry was still making a very active effort to unseat me, and I found myself occasionally sitting outside his house late at night in my now dented truck, contemplating nonspecific acts of violence and passively directing every ounce of my abundant rage toward his front door. And it scares me now to think of how I behaved, how close I must have been to some perilous unseen edge; it scares me to think, to know I can, or at least *could* feel and act the way I did.

Strangely, I don't remember my final sad departure from Nancy and Wichita. Perhaps it's because I don't really want to. I only remember thinking there might still be a distant possibility that we could somehow eventually reconstruct that which was so violently destroyed.

I was wrong of course. I often am. At least that is what I tell myself now.

21

EST

On my way back to New York, in a misguided effort to somehow fill the gaping hole that had been rent in my soul, I stopped in Muncie to search for Carolyn. I actually telephoned her ex-husband when I arrived, posing as a representative of a bank or something equally improbable. Although he didn't have her phone number, he did trustingly provide me with her new husband's name, Billy Larson. There was only one Bill Larson in the Muncie phonebook, so I tried to call first, and then, when there was no answer, I drove to the address listed in the phonebook. Twenty minutes later I found myself in front of a dilapidated one-story wooden shack in the heart of the Muncie slums. This was the address, but it couldn't be her home. Carolyn would not have been willing to live like this.

It wasn't until I got back to New York that I realized my error: Carolyn would have married a successful man—a man who would likely have been listed, not as Bill, but as William Larson. I immediately called long distance information and learned that I was right. William Larson was an attorney and Carolyn was happily and comfortably married. Although she seemed glad to hear from me when I finally reached her, she wasn't in a position to distract me from the love I had lost. And I guess I didn't really expect her to. I was just reaching out blindly, in grim desperation, for something, anything to hold on to.

In the following months, communications between Nancy and me became less frequent, and even more strained and uncomfortable. I truly loved her, and did not want to lose her, or, more accurately, to admit to myself that I already had, but there was something else—something beyond the grief of losing someone I loved so passionately. There was bitter anger and scorching pain that I think was strictly a function of some ancient loss. There was losing her, and there was losing that which I perceived as mine, losing love, and feeling rejected, and all of that ate away at me like a cancer. It was a very basic, primal feeling, like what I imagine a starving baby might feel, cruelly deprived of his mother's swelling nipple. Again.

Soon I began working with a married couple who owned instruments and microphones, and somehow, despite their utter incompetence, secured moderately profitable employment on occasional winter weekends in the Catskills. They would hire one of several female singers with whom they'd worked in the past, locate an available drummer, and then, without squandering a moment on rehearsal, show up in front of an unfortunate crowd of weary skiers to do considerable damage to the simplest popular music of the past and present, rendering it virtually unrecognizable. The man, a thirty-something, roly-poly, balding Richard Dryfuss type, imagined he could play bass and trumpet and sing, while the woman, a little overweight, though not hideously unattractive, stood statue-like, making offensive ululations behind a cheap electronic Casio keyboard programmed for aural assault. Once again, I was filled with shame.

The first of the various singers I encountered with this band was a fairly attractive, large-breasted woman on whom I might have made halfhearted advances if it hadn't been for her religious refusal to shave her ape-like legs. It was obvious that Davida liked me, and I tried to talk myself into visiting her room late at night when I found myself gripping an anxious erection, but I just couldn't do it. And the truth is that I couldn't stop thinking about Nancy, so far away, and receding farther every day.

But then...

A couple weeks later, when I showed up at the couple's house just north of Manhattan, I met Alexandra, a taller, far more attractive young woman who bore no resemblance whatsoever to our hairier primate cousins.

It was snowing hard that night, and we weren't at all certain we could even make it to the small resort near the peak of Hunter Mountain, but after some deliberation, we all agreed to attempt it. Our tone-deaf leaders led the way through the blizzard in their own car, while Alexandra rode with me. As we slipped and slid through the escalating storm, Alex proudly described her recent "enlightening experiences" with EST, a popular, cult-like, underground pseudo-religion that had a limited but avid following among artists, musicians, Californians, and even a few relatively normal people. While we climbed past cars and buses abandoned along the banks of the treacherous mountain road, she explained, with convincing calm, that there had been a time, not too long ago, when she would have been a nervous wreck in such harrowing conditions. She would have been quivering, or hiding under the seat, she said, but now, thanks to the profound influence of her newfound "religion," she was comfortable, and perfectly at ease.

I had always been enormously skeptical of such things, but I thought she'd made a fairly persuasive argument until, when we finally arrived at the snow-blanketed resort, I looked over at her tightly clenched hands and watched her struggle to ply them apart. Blood dripped from the backs of both hands as she drew her fingernails, one by one, from the gaping wounds she'd "calmly" drilled. Nevertheless, I really liked her, and was not disappointed when we learned that we would have to share a room, and a bed.

As I recall, Alexandra was not a terrible singer, and she had a very good attitude (for my devious and dissolute purposes) about such things as cohabitation. She seemed not even a little ill at ease with the idea of sharing a room and a bed with me. And though I could not get Nancy out of my mind and heart, other fierce drives were making a valiant effort in their campaign to obscure her memory, even if only for a while.

So…

Back in our tiny room that night, with the degrading cacophony behind us, Alexandra and I spoke about our lives and loves. She described a boyfriend about whom she seemed to care, and I told her about darling distant Nancy. Later, when Alexandra heard me urinating after the shower I took to peel the scent of smoke from my skin and hair after our long night in the bar, she called through the door.

"Why didn't you just piss in the shower?"

"Huh?"

"Why didn't you just piss in the shower?"

"It really never occurred to me," I shouted back, a little embarrassed.

"I guess that makes sense," she said. You get to piss standing up whenever you want. I can't, so I like to do it in the shower."

When she emerged a half hour later, after her own shower, I was stretched out on the floor.

"What are you doing down there," she asked, apparently assuming I was being chivalrous.

"It occurred to me that you probably don't often get to shit lying down either."

She laughed as I slipped into bed next to her, still begrudgingly keeping a respectful distance.

For a while we lay next to each other, chatting like old friends. But soon we began to discuss, very logically and maturely, the possibility of yielding to our animal instincts. We liked each other, we swiftly resolved, but we needed to consider the feelings of the people we loved. But whom would it hurt, we asked one another, and my body began to respond to the intimate discussion and the proximity of this tall, alluring, not to mention smooth-legged woman. Eventually, after inching slowly nearer to one another, we agreed that it wouldn't be right, no matter how much we wanted it. Damn.

I was about to wish her a goodnight when she turned toward me and whispered, "But if you want to, you can masturbate."

"I am. I have been," I confessed, and she reached over to offer her deft assistance.

"So am I," she responded, her voice shaking sensually as I came all over myself and her gentle, agreeable hand.

"You taste good," she said, after licking her fingers.

I think we should both be very proud of the restraint we exercised.

At the end of our short stay we talked about getting together again, but unfortunately, I guess, it never materialized.

I suppose it was inevitable that Nancy would eventually want me to return the truck she had bought for me. Nevertheless, it hurt my feelings and caused me serious inconvenience and expense. Suddenly I was in desperate need of more regular work.

22

"Arzairenymeninzeesroomtoon atuh?"

F inding work, particularly full-time work, as a musician, is seldom
easy. A lot of it is done through word of mouth, but for that to be
effective you have to actually know and talk to other musicians. And
the best work is snatched up rapidly. There is always the Musicians'
Union, but in my experience this is one of the weakest, most ineffec-
tual organizations extant. And in some cities there are, or were twenty
years ago, musicians' referral services that charged small fees to put you
in contact with people who were ostensibly looking for someone with
your alleged skills. Still, however you approach it, it can be a tedious
and very frustrating process.

I didn't know a lot of people in New York, and I didn't have much
time or money. I had earned several hundred dollars through the reluctant sale of my old Marvel comic book collection—for which, inciden-
tally, I could have gotten much more if not for my sense of
urgency—but that money wouldn't last long in the city. I found my
next band through a want ad in the Village Voice, a weekly New York
newspaper with a following among the young and theoretically hip.

Wanted: Drummer for highly professional working show band.
Good pay, immediate work. Must be willing to travel. Vocals and ability to read music a plus. Call Michelle or Dave, etc.

Michelle was an aging French performer (of course we're all aging,
but she had a substantial head start) with no real skills outside of the
ones she'd undoubtedly employed to obtain the financial backing

119

required to put a band together and pay for rehearsals. Dave was her much younger, guitar owning boyfriend, and, as I would soon learn, a complete, woman-abusing asshole. I auditioned and they hired me on the spot—lucky me. Lucky them.

The bass player, yet another in a long line of Steves, I think, was skinny, long-faced, and, relatively untalented, but harmless. And the keyboard player, Mike, I think, had studied music at Oberlin College with my brother Christopher, and was capable but a little distracted and terminally uninspired by the music we were slaughtering. And then there were the two dancers/singers, Frank, I think, and Greg, I think, nice enough guys, I think, and apparently in love, but with precious nothing to offer in the way of musical inspiration. This was not going to be, for me, a labor of love.

So after two weeks of paid rehearsals, during which I somehow became the band's vocal arranger, we set out for Miami Beach, where we were booked for six weeks in The Boom Boom Room at the once (a long, long time ago) glamorous, Hotel Fontainebleau. Fortunately, we embarrassed ourselves for only a couple hours a night, which meant plenty of leisure time during the day to lay in the sun, getting dark and planning for a cancerous and leathery future, and at night, after we'd finished, to walk on the beach or go out to the other not-so-hot spots along Miami Beach's once (a long, long time ago) bustling Collins Avenue.

Although I was still writing to Nancy, still entertaining gradually dwindling hopes, and still wallowing in the sorrow I'd come to know so well, I occasionally went out in futile, lonely search of whatever it was I was searching for. Unfortunately, my early efforts were not as productive as I would have liked.

About the shows…

After a couple of standard-issue dance tunes, Dave would garble the overexcited announcement for "the fabulous Michelle Frasconi." At that point Michelle would come prancing awkwardly out from behind the red velvet curtain and moan a poorly constructed medley of old show tunes, while Frank and Greg, draped in the silliest of sequined polyester jumpsuits, kicked and strutted like Rockettes around the perimeter of the stage. Dave, having wisely sneaked safely off stage during this embarrassing exhibition, would stand behind the curtain, waiting with childlike eagerness until I announced, "the King of rock and roll, Elvis Presley."

When Dave's disgraceful display of ineptitude finally came to an anticlimactic but welcome end, Michelle would reappear for the audience participation section of the blunder. While we vamped monotonously, she would ask the dumbstruck audience in the thickest, most incomprehensible accent imaginable, "Arzairenymeninzeesroomtoonatuh?"

No response.

"Arzairenymeninzeesroomtoonatuh?" She would try a second time.

Then, after three or four or more failed attempts, she would slow it down, "Are Zair eneemen in zees room toonat uh?"

Finally, someone would catch on, spoiling our fun; she was looking for men. Inevitably, though I'll never understand why, a few elderly men would hobble up to the stage, where they would stand embarrassed and deeply confused, grinning stupidly back at their stupidly grinning wives as Michelle asked, "Djoonoatoodoozufwanshcahngcahng?"

Silence.

"Djoonoatoodoozufwanshcahngcahng?"

Uncomfortable silence.

"Djoonoatoodoozufwanshcahngcahng?"

Hilarious, bewildered, extremely uncomfortable silence.

"Du Joo no atoodoo zee Fwransch cahng cahng?"

Usually, one of the spoilsports would decipher it and explain it to the others, at which time Michelle would attempt to teach them to do the ridiculous fucking French cancan, which, even if she had communicated her requests in something less than twenty-five tedious minutes, would have been about as entertaining as, well, as it sounds.

And Dave's Elvis impersonation sucked. He simply sang, in his own weak, unexceptional voice, a poorly constructed medley of tired, no, *exhausted* Elvis hits. I was learning the *real* meaning of shame. It's funny to think that, having played with this travesty right on the heels of that debacle in the Catskills, I had any self-respect left at all. I remember explaining to my father, when rethinking my career years later, that I could never work in a department store, that I would just be too ashamed. What the fuck was I thinking? "A pair of the red pumps in a seven? No problem...sir."

And...

One warm afternoon during our stay in Miami Beach, as we paced along the diminishing shoreline behind the aging hotel, Steve and I met and swiftly befriended two young women, one with a very pretty face but a little overweight, the other with a nearly perfect body and a not unattractive though not beautiful face. Perfectly proportioned Harriet and her plump but pretty friend were from Long Island. They had come to Florida to escape their parents and boyfriends, and in eager search of the sun and meaningless sex. They had, we assured them, come to the right place. And Harriet and I had good clean fun together in my room, in the other unoccupied rooms to which I gained illegal access, and at night on the balmy beach. Although I could never call her by her unfortunate, ill-chosen name, I was glad we'd found each other. Regrettably, after a week of good-natured frolicking, the two nymphs had to return to New York. So, desperate and bored again, I did the only thing that made any sense: I bought a used motorcycle.

At night after work I would ride north to Orlando, sometimes alone, and sometimes with one of my fellow sufferers. And during the day, usually alone, I'd travel south to the Keys or west into the Everglades, where I might just stroll along with only the slightest distant hope of meeting the next, one and only love of my life. Although I often enjoyed my restless travels, not one of these excursions was successful in terms of my major focus.

At some point toward the end of our stay in Miami Beach, I had a brief visit from Gail Ginelli, a girl from Newark whom I'd met and slept with on one of those dull winter weekends at Hunter Mountain. But Gail, as nice as she was, was just another temporary distraction; after all, she was from Newark. Even more disconcerting than her pedestrian provenance, though, was the fact that one night, seconds after I exploded in a writhing, screaming, and vigorous orgasm (one that nearly unseated her, jettisoning her through the wall and into the next room), she looked down at me and asked dizzily, "Did you sperm?" First of all, the only other possible explanation for my behavior would have been a massive fatal coronary, in which case I would have been spared the idiotic question, secondly, and possibly more important, sperm is a *noun*, not a fucking *verb*.

And then…

Late one night, days after Gail's timely departure, Mike's girlfriend, who had also come to visit, making our shared quarters more than a little crowded, mysteriously disappeared. Mike and I waited for several uneasy hours before we began to panic. But then, very early in the morning, we panicked quite effectively, pacing for miles in both directions on the dark deserted beach in frantic search of her, or her bloody remains. It wasn't until the following afternoon, after a sleepless night, that she reappeared, as yet unharmed, but working on it. She had spent the night with some guy she'd met in the hotel. And the fucking gee-bah confessed!

The next morning Mike's ex-girlfriend flew back to New York, and two days later, heartbroken but still foolishly hopeful, Mike gave his notice, giving us just enough time to replace him with a friendly and reasonably competent keyboard player from Scotland, probably named Duncan.

Suddenly we had to rehearse again, which meant taking time away from my nearly perfect tan, spending time with the other members of the band, and getting to know them better than I'd ever wanted to.

Despite his absolute paucity of musical facility, Dave perceived himself as the bandleader, which might have been tolerable if he'd kept the absurd delusion to himself. But when he actually tried to take control of the rehearsals, flexing his impotent muscles and making idiotic suggestions, the situation became unbearable for all of us. This was a manchild who, without my assistance, could not have played, even poorly, the elementary guitar line from a too popular Bee Gees song we were learning. I actually sat with him for over an hour, repeatedly playing the insipid pentatonic melody that I'd learned seconds earlier without effort on Steve's bass. The angry idiot stared at me as though I were speaking in his battered girlfriend's exaggerated accent. And this same worthless, woman beating bag of vomit, at the next rehearsal, frustrated at my obstinate unwillingness to cooperate with a truly moronic direction, shrieked, "Drummers aren't even musicians."

"Gee Dave," I said with quiet sarcasm, "what do you think it says about *you*, that a lowly, dull-witted, non-musician drummer had to teach you that amazingly elementary guitar part that you still can't play for sour apple shit?"

He stormed out of the room.

And that night, when it came time to introduce the "king of rock and roll," I made a critical decision, which I was about to express in my announcement. "And now, ladies and gentlemen," I proclaimed in my most enthusiastic, over-the-top, Las Vegas announcer's voice, "lets have an apathetic round of indignation for the king of rock and roll, Miss Shirrrrrrrrrrrrrrrrrrrrrrrrrrrrley Temple."

And Dave had no choice but to stroll out and mangle his stupid Elvis medley.

Oh yeah, and I quit.

Oh yeah, and so did everyone else.

So...

I mounted my new used Honda 450 and headed north once again, this time to Pennsylvania, where I planned to visit my mother and some old friends. My colleagues from the band were kind enough to deliver my drums to me on their way to back New York the following week.

23

You Can Go Home…But I Really Don't Recommend it

Back in Pennsylvania I stayed with my old childhood buddies, Bert and Joe, who then shared a profoundly disordered and dirty apartment in Delaware Water Gap. They were kind enough to offer me the couch, which reeked, as did the entire apartment, of cigarettes, beer, vomit (I assume), and a mysterious medley of objectionable body odors. Despite all of that, I decided to stay for a little while before calling Larry Lovejoy in Boston to see if he or anyone he knew was looking for a drummer, singer, comedian, vocal arranger, and all around hostile lunatic.

But shortly after my return to Pennsylvania I was informed of an opening in the house band at Fernwood, the only Pocono resort at which I had ever played. Those of you who can recall things you've never actually known will remember that I worked there with Fred Waring Junior in the few weeks before our first road trip, and several times shortly thereafter with *The Jarrett Brothers' Band*. So I strolled in early one evening with helmet in hand and I played and sang exceptionally poorly throughout the uncomfortable twenty-minute live audition. The bandleader, a perceptive and quite gifted saxophonist who went by the unexplained nickname of Tee, was not impressed, but the oversized middle-aged female singer, who was sleeping with the ancient married owner of the resort, apparently thought I was talented and charming, and soon I was hired. Though I still expected to leave for Boston within weeks, or months at the most, I decided to take the job in order to earn some much-needed money in the meantime.

Again, it is interesting (I hope) what we remember after so much time has passed. Of course I remember getting drunk with my old friends and riding my motorcycle recklessly around the winding back roads, and I remember having sex on the golf course next to Bert and Joe's rancid apartment building with some girl who I vaguely recalled from my earlier years in Pennsylvania, and who from that night on I would remember only as "the nineteenth hole." I remember too a brief visit from Harriet, who seemed disturbed for some reason by the fact that I now had a regular income and consequently no longer fit the image she'd had of a struggling artist living day to day. But the most potent memory of my brief stay with Bert and Joe is that of my mother's bizarre behavior when I was vainly battling a nasty cold, or flu (I'm *still* not certain I can tell the difference).

We'd had dinner together that evening at a local diner, and I was sneezing and sniffling uncontrollably as she drove me back to the apartment. But when I reached back to take a handful of tissues from the full box that for as long as I can remember she's kept on the shelf above the back seat, she looked over at me and asked, "How many do you need?"

"Uh, I don't know," I said. "Just enough to get me through the night, I guess." I suppose I was expecting her to offer the entire box.

"Well *jeez*, Grant," she whined, visibly frustrated and upset, "that's the only box of Kleenex I *have*. I'd really prefer it if you only took one or two."

My mother was physically healthy, with no apparent urgent need for a large quantity of tissue; she had a decent job, she ate well, and I had often sent her money during my time on the road, but, well, by gosh, that was the only box of Kleenex she *had*. Yikes. And if I were foolish enough to remind her of the event today, she would deny it most emphatically. My mother has her own special and, it seems, very effective way of dealing with pain and shame and the many things she now probably wishes had never occurred.

24

Now That's Entertainment

Initially I hadn't planned to spend a lot of time in Pennsylvania. But having found a passable job that paid relatively well—a job wherein, for the first time in many years, I would not have to pack up and move all my worldly possessions every couple weeks—and having received only a very vague, tentative response from my old friend, Larry, I found myself slowly, and quite unexpectedly settling in.

So I bought myself a pretty, new, blue Toyota pickup truck with custom wheels and a fiberglass top, and, with my friend Brett, rented a house in Rosetto, a small and unusual community comprised exclusively of large, close-knit, Italian-American families and their large, close-knit, Italian-American progeny. It is actually possible that Brett and I were the only people not of Italian descent ever permitted to live in this community. We may also have been the only inhabitants over the age of ten who weighed less than 275 pounds fully clothed.

Years earlier, as you may recall, after Fred Waring Jr., and before Boston, Brett and I had shared an apartment in Manhattan, where we worked together at an ad agency and played together in *The Bob Lenox Trio*. Outside of a few relatively minor disagreements and a couple of ugly (and permanently scarring) rubber band battles, we got along quite well. He was and is a shy, gentle man. I have happily remained in contact with him in the years since. We were probably both very fortunate to have each other again as housemates.

Brett played with various local bands, and I worked five or six easy nights a week at Fernwood. And in our spare time, we, along with Eric Doney, a keyboard player with whom I'd played in a jazz trio at the tender age of fifteen, worked together on my brother Scott's perpetual imaginary "album" project.

Meanwhile...

When I accepted the job at Fernwood with *Tee and Company*, I was told that I might, on rare occasion, be expected to employ the music reading skills to which I had indirectly and somewhat dishonestly alluded during the brief informal interview that followed my audition. Whatever negligible reading skills I'd cultivated in the distant past had faded long ago into the recesses of my embattled memory. I had fully expected to be gone long before I would ever be called upon to demonstrate these alleged skills, and figured that if the unexpected situation *did* in fact arise during my brief stay I could get by relying on my ear, or that, in the worst case, I could learn very quickly to read.

To my astonishment and relief, the first show that required reading was the comedy team of Dick Chase and Bud Mitchell—the two petulant clowns with whom I'd gone on the road years before. Fortunately for me, if not for the audience, they were still trudging through the same tired routine with the same music. From what I was able to discern, they were also engaging in the same arguments. Although the charts made little sense to me at this point, I remembered every note and, for that matter, every idiotic word of their show, which made me appear to be quite proficient. And had that been the only show for which I would have to read, I would have been an unqualified success. Unfortunately, there was another, completely unfamiliar show booked for the following Saturday night, affording me exactly one week to learn to read music.

June Valley, whose name then meant nothing to me, and now means little, was at one time, according to legend, a popular singer. She was nice enough, but she brought along with her, her annoying, sax playing husband and bandleader, "Greasy Jimmy Whatever." Jimmy was not a terrifically gifted man; he was also not a patient man. And though I was able, after an extended tense rehearsal and an evening of studying the charts and listening to the rehearsal tapes, to struggle through the show without causing any serious injuries, it became obvious that I was going to have to learn to sight-read.

It was that information, driven home by a powerful lifetime aversion to self-induced shame, in addition to the bandleader's gentle coaxing and the prospect of more interesting work with Scott and others, that led me to the uncharacteristically mature conclusion that this might be a good time to actually learn to play my chosen instrument. Merciful heavens! And so it was that I began to practice. It is truly amazing what just a little interest and enthusiasm, combined with a lot of free time and some hint of natural ability, can do. After working as a professional drummer for ten years, I was finally learning to play the drums. Duh.

Now please don't get the wrong impression. I wasn't abandoning my true priorities; I was simply branching out a little, exploring alternate lifestyles. And I guess I was beginning to become aware of the vague, distant possibility that I would eventually have to at least *act* like an adult—a truly daunting prospect, and one that I would continue to stave off with relative success in virtually every other way imaginable for a long time to come.

Some basic information…

Fernwood, where despite myself I was swiftly becoming more and more at home, was and is a sprawling vacation resort that consumes a broad swath of Route 209 between Stroudsburg and Bushkill in Northeastern Pennsylvania's Pocono Mountains. It was a place where families and couples, mostly middle aged and older, the great majority of them from Eastern New Jersey and Long Island, went, ostensibly to get away from all the other middle-aged and older families and couples from Eastern New Jersey and Long Island who also went there presumably for the same reason. It was virtually the same group, though somewhat paler perhaps, that you might have encountered on a Sunday afternoon at the Bergen mall. There were also senior citizen outings and high school classes and a seedy variety of surprised and disappointed groups who'd been condemned by some cost-cutting entertainment director to a night or a week of sub-life at the uninspiring roadside resort.

Tee and Company was, when I began my sentence, a quartet made up of Tee on Alto Sax and Flute, Mark Homzik on Hammond B-3 and ancient synthesizer, Bobby Dodelin on electric bass, over-sized ego, and saccharine vocals, and me. The band's vocalist, Julie, would sing an occasional song during the dance sets, but her capacious lungs were mostly reserved for the shows and the humjobs I assume she administered to "owner Bob."

Tee, a tall, dark-complected man with a neat mustache and a notable if variable stomach, is now a very successfully recovering alcoholic. Unfortunately, he was not even beginning to recover when we first started working together. Mark, who was at least as crude and charmless as he appeared, was big and unwieldy, with slowly receding, long, dirty-brown hair, and an excess of uncombed facial fur. And Bobby, a reasonably good bass player whose reign with the organization was fortunately brief, was about as attractive as Barry Manilow might be with a human nose, and possessed a somewhat similar voice. He also appeared to be extremely uncomfortable having another vaguely appealing young man around to soak up some of the female attention he seemed certain belonged exclusively to him. I can remember on several occasions hearing him explain to people, mostly female type people, how much better his singing was than mine. It was probably true, but *jeez*.

Given the limited demographics of the customer base, my prospective 'mating' options at the resort were generally restricted to employees and the odd, ill-placed daughter of an unsuspecting vacationing family. Had I been more open-minded, my tastes wider ranging, I might have had considerable success with the over sixty-five group too, who for some reason, seemed quite fond of me. Though I never acted on the impulse, I often considered asking one or another of the friendly geezers or dowagers if they had any available granddaughters for me to molest. Fortunately there was a constantly changing group of virginal waiters and waitresses—the latter giving me a pool from which to choose—and a somewhat less fluid series of hostesses to add to the mix.

The band, in its various configurations, was always more effective performing jazz standards and ballads than top-forty, pop, or rock. We had no guitar and we weren't kids, but we did a reasonably good job with the music we knew, and we developed a mildly to very enthusiastic following, particularly among the ballroom dancers in the audience. Cha-cha-cha.

And oh what a bizarre cast of characters were assembled around us at the Pocono Mountain resort. Bob and Harvey Arnt, the two elderly owners of the complex, gave proof to the hypothesis that there is no relationship whatsoever between wealth, and style or character. To be completely fair I will admit that Bob, the one who was enjoying an extramarital affair with our blimp-like singer, and certainly the more likeable of the two, was always nice to me and had some redeeming qualities. But Harvey and his pudgy, oinking son, Pervis, were both hostile and exceedingly unpleasant. I hated them.

Chip, the bar manager, was a tall, dark, and somehow confusing looking man. He sported a thick black moustache and an unconvincing matching hairpiece, and had a dry, caustic sense of humor. Frank, his second in command, was apparently more comfortable with his own hair loss and was quite pleasant in an avuncular sort of way. Working alongside the two of them were Bobby, a bulky younger man—with lots of his own real dark hair and his own genuine thick moustache—who was also an aspiring alcoholic, and Mike, who also tended toward bulk and who generally treated me reasonably well. I would later learn that they were all, or almost all, "allegedly" robbing the place blind. Oh my.

Vivian, an eternal fixture at Fernwood, was almost indescribable, but I'll try just for the exercise. She was about five feet tall with an ass at least as wide and just about that many teeth. She did not walk, she waddled around the halls, swearing and complaining like some horrible ugly mole with a hippo's butt and a terminal case of Tourette's syndrome. She was possibly the most faithful employee the resort possessed, though I could never quite figure out what it was that she did, outside of spreading gossip and reporting to the authorities even the tiniest infraction perpetrated by any of the human employees. I think she and her formidable ass held camp in her crowded old Dodge station wagon.

And...

There were other "entertainers." "Ragtime Charlie Young" played during the band's breaks in the Gaslight Lounge, sitting in full costume behind his custom, genuine, new, old-time piano thing, telling not very funny, vaguely dirty jokes and grunting the songs that were bad fifty years before, sometimes making up his own puerile lyrics. For instance: "Tiny boobies, hiding in your brar; tiny boobies, I wonder where the hell they are." It is possible that the resort was actually built around Charlie. And he was *always* trying to tune that piece of shit piano. "Twang, twang."

Vince Jones was yet another very, very old man with a very, very bad hairpiece who played guitar and sang very, very, very old songs perched on a stool, conducting sing-a-longs and always, always ending his songs with the same two chords. Vince might have been a nice guy, but his wife, Bitch Jones, who would occasionally show up to make certain Vince was still breathing, was a nasty little racist shrew of a woman. I don't care *how* old she was. "Why don't they ever let a white guy win," was her insightful question when Mohammed Ali won his ninth or tenth well-earned heavyweight title.

On our nights off and on busy weekends, when Fernwood was able to support two bands, Joe Travers and his awful quartet, *Phase Phore* shamelessly butchered the worst of the top-forty and a carefully chosen collection of the less complex standards. Joe was a short, stocky weasel with a virulent case of little man's disease and a truly grating Sonny Bono "now where did that note go?" edge to his voice. He said and did all those things that you think of when you envision, if you are that unfortunate, a cheesy lounge singer saying and doing. He twirled his microphone from one paw to another, lowering half of his thick brown unibrow as he pranced around the tiny stage on cloven hooves, occasionally winking fiendishly at some poor terrified female in the usually stunned audience. I didn't care for him. And he had assembled a uniquely inept, poorly paid group of young unfortunates to support him in his ceaseless assault on harmony, melody, rhythm, and the tender human ear.

On certain nights, if you dared to walk the halls between the various rooms of torture, you had a fairly clear and frightening sense of what violent insanity might feel like from the inside—a hideous festival of smoke, noise and perspiration. And there was more to come.

So I played and sang and practiced and searched for new and interesting places to stick my pee-pee at the resort and in the local nightclubs, both after work and on my nights off. And although I never felt quite as comfortable in or near my hometown as I did elsewhere, I often found what I was looking for, or something reasonably close. And I continued working with Scott, recording his songs in a local studio, and beginning to feel more and more like a real live musician, in spite of the substantial evidence to the contrary.

25

Sex, Drugs, and Take Me to the Hospital

There was a pretty hostess and a cute waitress or two, and soon I met Terry, a bartender at "The Bottom of the Fox," a ramshackle bar at the bottom of Main Street in Delaware Water Gap that was owned by an angry, middle-aged social outcast who would go out early in the morning, after the bar had closed and all the drugs in the county had been ingested and absorbed, and shoot out the streetlights of the quaint little town with a high powered rifle. Ed liked Terry too, and had been pursuing her without success for a long time, but more about that later.

Terry was a nice person, I suppose, but she was also a perfect example of what we do in our obsessive search for love and sex. Okay, maybe she was only a perfect example of what *I* did in *my* obsessive search for love and sex. In any case, there was really no reason, outside of a shared loneliness, boredom, and mindless desperation, for us to be together. She was divorced and had a five-year-old daughter with whom she lived in a small apartment they shared with another addict about her age. Terry was overly fond, I thought, of pot and cocaine, substances in which I had no interest at all. In fact, despite my own occasional use, appreciation, and even abuse of alcohol, I had always been uncomfortable with the *other* drugs.

And there were other problems. Terry's cute daughter was hostile and jealous of me, and Terry had some mysterious underlying issues that came to the surface late at night. Occasionally, just after I'd finally dropped off to sleep, she would shoot up in bed and shriek in terror at some imaginary threat. "Aaaaaaaaaaaaaaaaaaaaaaaaaaaaakkk!" It was just so silly for both of us; she would get very high, I would get very angry, and her drug money would be wasted as she tumbled back to the ugly earth with a thud and a shriek.

I remember how Terry would sit beside me (once I'd adjusted to the idea of her pot-smoking) and, without fail, instinctively pass the stinky things toward me, forgetting for the moment either who I was or how I felt. And I remember too how I would say, without fail, "No thanks, I'm trying to quit," willing to beat any joke into the ground. But toward the end of our strange, strained relationship, weary of the monotonous routine, I decided to see if she would notice if I altered the pattern.

We were sitting together that night, mindlessly gazing at something idiotic on her television as we had so many nights before, when Terry lit a joint. After her first long drag she passed it to me, but this time, instead of my usual response, I accepted it without comment, drew deeply, held in the toxic smoke, and passed it back to her. When she didn't notice, mechanically offering it to me a second time, I took it, thanked her, and filled my traumatized lungs once more. Together, within minutes, we finished the evil weed. She realized nothing until she saw the bewildered expression that had seized my countenance.

I don't know what it was that I smoked that evening, and I doubt that she did either, but my carefully controlled world was changing rapidly. "I feel a little peculiar," was what I was trying to say, when what emerged was, "Myurna voot reemanama mamanama pl."

"Are you alright," she asked, and her head grew wider and wider.

"I want to go to the hospital now," was my next intended message. What I believe came out this time was, "Fuverumunk plambl merm-ermermermeroooo."

Then things got a little weird. I stood up, folded my long floppy ears back, and glanced down at Terry, who was pulling an angry schnauzer out of the top of her broad, rubbery forehead as three of her yellow eyes bulged insidiously. Finally, I did the only thing I could think of. I asked her one more time to take me to the hospital, pronouncing each word very, very carefully, "Bububub, bub" before braving the rapidly deteriorating staircase and taking a walk in the sticky green rain.

It was at about five o'clock the following morning when I wakened to see Ed standing outside Terry's bedroom door, apparently deep in thought and holding his high-powered rifle at his side. At first I made the entirely reasonable assumption that this was simply a residual hallucination from the evening's illicit activities. But when he refused to grow horns or turn into a flounder I began to suspect that he was really there. In nervous silence, I waited as Ed peered into the bedroom and brought his weapon into what looked to me like aiming and firing and killing me position. He just stood motionless for a frightening minute before turning and strolling away. To this day I believe Ed, undoubtedly in a drunken, drug-induced haze, was contemplating my murder.

As it happened, Ed was murdered outside his bar just a year or so later by someone with a powerful arm, a large axe, and a strong stomach. Yuck.

The moral of this story of drug abuse, for you kids out there, is, just say "merma nerma merma nerma pl."

26

Hideous Fashion Syndrome

Shortly after Terry and I parted I noticed a lovely girl who was staying with her family at the resort. After flirting with her night after night for almost a week, I finally sat down next to her on the bench in the hall between the noises from hell and asked her to marry me. It was on her last night there, a few nights later, following the skillful hand job she performed in the front seat of my pickup truck, that I learned that she was "almost fifteen." I swear I had no idea. And in my defense, I just want to say that I deliberated long and very hard before driving to Queens weeks later to pick her up and bring her back across state lines to Pennsylvania, where I resumed my reprehensible criminal endeavor. Brett may have been a little put-off when he realized my houseguest's age, but he didn't really show it, and I think I appreciate it. I believe her name was Felony.

And soon...

Bobby, our dip-shit bass player, quit the band to go to finishing school or get toilet training or something, and Brett was hired to work with us on weekends (on weeknights Mark now played pedal bass on his organ, saving the resort precious money and making my life even more miserable). I fucked the hotel photographer and a couple of waitresses, all of whom were completely legal, I think, and life went on in the same old way for a while. Tee's drinking increased and he married the ex-wife of the homosexual son of Bob Arnt, the more palatable of the two hotel owners, happily acquiring in the process three adorable, if somewhat confused, kids. Kids who, by the way, are all doing exceptionally well today. I know this because they are still my friends. Hey, I can't believe it either.

Tee and Company played behind *The Four Aces, The Four Lads*, Soupy Sales, and a bizarre cast of had-beens, had-almost-beens, and never-had-a-chance-in-hell-of-beings. I was still improving, still practicing, and still trying not to take life too seriously—the latter no great effort. I discovered an interest in photography and began occasionally sitting-in on drums after hours in the local jazz clubs. A new staff of waitresses was soon hired and soon I encountered Karen, a perky, college student who was waiting on tables to earn some extra money and who seemed completely uninterested in me. I remember telling Brett one night, before I gathered the nerve to actually proposition the tall, well-formed brunette with the amazingly gooey laugh, that I simply had to have her. After a couple weeks of firm and convincing rejections she began to waver.

Around the same time, I befriended Greg, a waiter at the resort who, in addition to his interest in drumming and photography, was smitten with Irene, a part-time waitress who had developed a close friendship with Karen. When Irene suggested a double date, Karen halfheartedly capitulated. We had a decent dinner that evening, and afterwards we went out to listen to a local jazz band. I think we all had a fairly good time, but there was a problem—I was suffering a horrific relapse of the "hideous fashion syndrome" that I'd caught from Larry (or he'd caught from me) years before. After all I've confessed about my life and my career, this may be the most difficult disclosure. I wore, that night, a very shiny, silver polyester shirt. And that's not all, though God knows I wish it were. It had very shiny silver polyester tassels—lots of them, hundreds of them, maybe thousands!—and pearl snaps. Yee-ha! It is a miracle that Karen got into the car in the first place and even more astonishing that she accepted my request for a second date. What the fuck was *her* problem?

So…

Karen and I went out again and Scott signed an exclusive management contract with Joel Yooguysereelyfuktnow. Joel told Scott he wanted the entire band to sign with him and Scott brought us the contracts to read and sign. I recall sitting with Brett in our living room, examining the documents, and realizing that, although there was no guarantee *Joel* would ever do *any*thing for *us*, he would be receiving twenty percent of any work of any kind that any one of us did for the next hundred years or so. "Hmm," I said to Brett and to myself. "I'm not sure this is completely fair. Hmm." Scott, in the end, was the only one who signed. Hmm.

For reasons I don't now recall, Brett and I gave up our house in Rosetto, and I moved in alone to a small, furnished basement apartment in a home in Henryville. Lore, who owned and still owns the home, is a very sweet German-born woman who treated me like a beloved member of her family. She was rarely around during the week, and not always there on weekends, but when she was there I was offered meals, and I was always invited to visit her and her friends upstairs. I quickly became very comfortable. And I must say, in atypical fairness, that if it weren't for my mother, who had been renting the apartment before me, and who apparently moved out so that I could live there, I would not have found such agreeable or inexpensive accommodations. That almost makes up for the tissue incident, but not quite.

But as pleasant as my living situation was, there were a few problems. The décor of my new apartment, with the notable exception of the set of drums that virtually consumed the living room, reflected the taste of a middle-aged German woman, from the little ceramic knick-knacks on the shelves to the drapes, the thick pile carpet and the furniture. It was not necessarily poor taste; it simply had nothing to do with me (which now that I think of it, with the image of that shiny silver shirt still etched in my mind, might not have been such a terrible thing). The other issue was that my privacy was compromised whenever Lore and her friends were around. She and many of her guests chose to come and go through the door that connected the garage to my kitchen, where there was a staircase leading to her home.

The first time Lore made an unexpected appearance, Karen and I were sitting on the couch, sharing a bottle of wine, listening to music, and gently groping one another. It was the sudden noisy rattle of the electric garage door that alerted us to Lore's arrival. We quickly got ourselves in order, and when Karen's heart rate, which seconds earlier I'd been monitoring with my tongue, returned to normal, I introduced her to Lore. About ten minutes later Lore called down to offer us some cookies, which she then brought down, politely leaving us alone afterwards and for the remainder of the evening. Karen and I were unusually subdued in our nocturnal activities that night, and in the morning as we prepared to depart we remained cautious not to be heard. Although it was technically none of her business, I liked Lore, and I wasn't sure how she would react to my overnight guest. I didn't want to upset her or risk jeopardizing my accommodations. But just as we were about to sneak out, she called down. "Grant, would you like some coffee?"

"No thanks," I responded, as I always did.

A silent second passed. "Karen, would *you* like some coffee?"

27

The Belly Dancer and the Record Deal

For a while Karen and I continued dating, sustaining what was ostensibly a monogamous relationship, and although we had fun, and our sexual relationship was rewarding, I don't think I ever felt terribly close to her. During the week, when she was away at school, I missed her, but by the time she arrived early Friday evening, I always found myself wishing one of us would leave. For some reason I was much fonder of her in her absence than when she was present. We laughed and fucked and sucked and played with vibrators and mutual masturbation and we probably even shared a little of ourselves, but I never became as emotionally intimate with Karen as I had with some of the women with whom I'd done many of the same things in the past. And I was certainly no more faithful to her than I had been to anyone before her.

Perhaps I had unknowingly transferred some tiny portion of my obsession with women (and girls) to other interests and endeavors, to practicing and playing music. I was still obsessed with sex of course, but possibly expending just a little of my limited energy in other areas. And it is likely, or possible at least, that I had sustained so much emotional damage in my stormy relationship with Nancy, and those few before her who actually mattered as much as I'd believed they did, that I was subconsciously protecting myself from the possibility of further injury. I *do* believe that the after-effects of that relationship were dramatic and extensive, and that some of my behavior, at that time and for a long time after, was a response to those effects. Anyway, that's my theory. And if I'm correct it could reasonably be inferred that the pain of Nancy's departure made me a much better musician. And going one step further, just for the hell of it, maybe I would have been even better if she had hurt me more. Bitch.

So let's see, I had my own inexpensive apartment with a backyard and a sunny deck, a young, libidinous girlfriend with firm, well-shaped parts in all the proper locations, a regular (and easy) job, a new truck, the prospect of more interesting musical work, and plenty of time to practice and masturbate. I probably should have been a happy guy. Oh well.

One of the more peculiar tasks our band was required to perform on occasional weekends was to play for one of several belly dancers the resort employed to make the shows even longer and more bizarre. They were an interesting variety of local women who had discovered that they could earn a couple hundred dollars on a Saturday night by dressing up in ridiculous costumes, strutting around, and acting foolish for twenty minutes or so. Most of them, I think, understood how silly their "work" was, though there were one or two who took it extremely seriously, bringing complex charts, tapes, and in one case, even a would-be conductor who patiently instructed us on how to play his girlfriend's "difficult" music "more effectively." The fucking jerk. And, as you might expect, the ones who were the most serious about the idiotic business were also the least capable.

When I was fifteen years old my older brother Eric had a very desirable girlfriend. Kelly, for whom I furtively lusted and with thoughts of whom I regularly abused myself, remained in friendly contact with my mother even after she'd stopped seeing Eric or he'd stopped seeing her. Kelly was smart and funny, and, of course, just a little odd—after all she'd remained in contact with my mother. She was the last person I expected to see when, on an otherwise unexceptional Saturday night, I met the new belly dancer, advertised on the marquis as "The Lovely Alethia." When I saw her in the hall before the show, still in her civilian attire, we just stared at each other in silence before our simultaneous recognition and the long embrace that followed. We talked for a couple minutes before she invited me into her dressing room, where we caught up with one another and laughed hard at the coincidence we'd shared. After the show Kelly invited me home with her, to hang out and talk. And yes, we did.

Over a period of several months Kelly and I had a mostly good time, and she was a lustful beast, shivering and shaking with repeated unexpected and apparently very powerful orgasms. I liked her, she liked me, and we did not fall in love. Still, it was truly wonderful to actually be able to fulfill the passionate childhood fantasy that I had long ago given up, if not forgotten. And she was happy, I think, to be a part of it. If there is a single reason, other than *my* involvement, for the "failure" of our relationship to become more than it did, it was probably that Kelly was still friendly with my mother. Or maybe it was that the fantasy always has fewer flaws than the reality. Or maybe she just didn't like me that much. Or whatever.

It was at around that time that I realized that my growing interest in photography might offer new ways of meeting and undressing beautiful women—not a particularly novel thought, but a profitable one, nonetheless. I soon found myself offering to take photographs of the more attractive women working or staying at the resort. And more than a couple of them were happy, or willing at least, to comply.

And after months of rehearsals and recording, the big break for which I'd been waiting finally came: Scott was offered a record deal. Manfred Eicher, with whom our older brother Keith had been recording for years, had heard the tapes and was ready to record our band for his label. Scott put him in touch with his manager, Joel, and Manfred made his simple, straightforward, and relatively generous offer. Joel was no fool though; he knew a good thing when he saw it, and he proceeded to talk Scott out of it, explaining that it was too easy, too uncomplicated. Scott should wait, he advised, for an offer that he could *really* fuck up. And Scott, as new to this ugly process as the rest of us, listened and complied, signing a deal months later with another label, a deal that resulted in an album that did not include the rest of the band and that really had nothing to do with his music, an album which ultimately died a quiet painful death, and, I'm sorry to say, deserved to. I guess Joel showed us.

The truth is that all of our lives would probably have been very different if Scott had ignored Joel's advice and signed with Manfred. I'm not certain anything would be better, but it would surely be different. Or not. And Scott never recorded a second album, which is a shame.

28

"You Gonna Know When the Song is Over"

Tee was slurring and wobbling as he'd never done before, and I was covering for his drunken incompetence, conducting the band from behind my drums while we all ignored his wildly flailing arms and confused grunts. And my friend, Brett, was moving on, or over, giving us the opportunity to hire some *real* talent. Oh my.

When we adopted Gerry Funkleman we didn't realize that in addition to gaining a truly mediocre (at best) bass player, we were getting one of the few living souls who could actually out-drink Tee in a head-to-head competition. And Gerry was way out in front when it came to idiotic behavior. He shared top billing in that area with yet another of the many alcoholics employed at Fernwood, Bungling Billy Forster.

Billy was the social director, which meant that he invented, or at least executed—a particularly apt term—the various games and activities used to keep the guests hiding in their dark, musty rooms. He was responsible for "name that tune," "musical trivia," "the funny hat contest" (my personal favorite), "the talent show," "horse racing" (using dice and tattered cardboard horses), "bingo" (that's how I want to spend *my* vacation), numerous headaches, and a number of other even more forgettable, mind numbing tortures. Maybe I can understand why he drank so much. But he was an asshole anyway.

Billy was also the worm who, during one of Tee's early doomed attempts to dry out, took Tee aside and confided, "Frankly, buddy, you were a lot more fun when you were drinking." When I learned of

his self-serving and amazingly insensitive comment, I told Billy that it
was okay with me if he wanted to drink himself to death, but that if he
ever said or did anything like that again to Tee, I would beat him into
an even punier lifeless pulp. He was surprisingly contrite.

So...

I continued to practice and to listen to the music that inspired me,
and my playing improved as a consequence. And despite my lack of
enthusiasm for most of the entertainment hired by the resort, I tried to
make the most out of the situation and to apply my developing skills to
whatever I was called upon to play.

For example...

One of the many musical groups with whom I was fortunate
enough to perform while working at Fernwood was *The Ink Spots*, a
quartet of singers that had had several big hits in the nineteen-fifties,
and had apparently spent most of their time since then, aging. When I
showed up for our Saturday afternoon rehearsal I was greeted by four,
very affable, elderly black men who seemed completely relaxed and
almost uninterested in our rehearsal. They'd brought their own bass
player, guitar player, and keyboard player, but needed a drummer to
complete the rhythm section. By this time I was quite comfortable
reading music, and I was happy to exercise and demonstrate my
improved skills, so when they told me that they had no charts, I was a
little disappointed, but not devastated. I had, after all, spent most of
my life playing by ear.

"Okay," I said from behind my drums, "who will be counting off
the tunes during the show?"

"We ain't gonna count 'em off. You just come in after a couple
bars," one of them said, with composure bordering on boredom.

"Just come in?"

"Yeah. Don't worry about it, it's all the same shit...that, uh, six-
eight or twelve-eight, or whatever. You know—'*Wong*, donga, dong,
Whack danga dang.' '*Wong*, donga, dong, *Whack* danga dang.'"

"Okay…alright, I can do that. What about breaks or, you know retards, things like that?"

"Nah, nah. Don't worry about it man. Maybe every once in a while you could put in a, uh, tympani roll or some kinda shit like that. You know."

"Sure, okay, but the endings are important, somebody's going to…uh…somebody's going to signal the endings, right?"

The wise old man just smirked at me like I was harshing his considerable mellow, and said very matter-of-factly, "Nah. You gonna know when the song is over…cause *we* all gonna stop *play*in'."

29

Dad Who?

And there was Billy Eckstine, to whom I had to apologize for Gerry's embarrassing incompetence, and Anna Maria Alberghetti, who sang quite well but seemed to believe she was still recognized by anyone under the age of dead as something more than the Good Seasons salad dressing saleswoman. Johnny Ray was old, legally deaf, and very loud, Soupy Sales was about as funny as you would expect, June Valley came back (her husband, Greasy Jimmy noticed and complimented me on my dramatic improvement, but I still didn't like him), and then there was Tony Martin.

Tony Martin had also been a very big name at some time in the distant past, but we were warned in anticipation of his arrival at Fernwood that there was a good chance he would either show up drunk or not at all. On the first of his two visits to the resort he forgot to bring his charts, and was, as advertised, very drunk, which simply meant that we all had to fake an entire show. The second time was a little different though. Tony remembered his charts, but forgot the rehearsal, which meant sight-reading an hour-long show behind an extremely inebriated man.

Things had been going just fine until about halfway through the show. He turned to the band and called a tune that required us to read a very intricate chart at warp speed. But despite the difficulty of the complex, break-neck piece, the band did an expert job, visibly relieved when we all ended together, aware that such a miraculous feat could never in our lifetimes be repeated. And although they were ignorant of the additional hardship with which we had been confronted, the audience roared, and Tony, moved to near sobriety by the impressive display of musicianship on our part, and appreciation on the part of the screaming audience, turned toward the weary, sweating band, and said with an 'erubescent smile, "What a great band. Aren't they a great band? Yeah, let's do it **one more time**." And we had to play the whole fucking horrible thing again.

I took semi-nude photographs of the new hostess, with whom I did not have sex, though I thought about it often until her sudden tragic death in an automobile accident on the way home from work late on New Years Eve. Just days after the accident I learned that her family had found some of the photographs I'd taken among the bits of abbreviated history she'd left behind. Though there was, in my opinion, nothing pornographic about the pictures, I was nervous and uneasy about what their reactions might be. But as it turned out they loved the photographs they found. A week or so later her brother visited the resort to thank me personally and ask if there were any others they could have. I didn't get to know Barbara very well, but I believe she was a nice young woman and her early death was certainly very sad.

And then there was the woman who worked at the front desk. Susan, with whom I would often flirt during the band's breaks, was not unattractive, but she was married, and far more importantly, she didn't really inspire my carnal instincts. But one night after work at The Big A, one of the bars I regularly passed and ignored on my way home, I found Susan sitting at a table with her friend, Mandy, and Susan's visiting cousin, don't know her name, don't care. Susan, who always seemed to enjoy flirting, invited me to join them, and the three of us sat talking, laughing, and drinking until the smoky bar closed.

It was probably a month or so later, at Fernwood, when I saw Mandy again. She was sitting with Susan at the bar in the Gaslight Lounge. I sat talking with them on our breaks, and when the band was finished, Susan invited me to join them for cocktails at her house. That night in Susan's living room I learned about Mandy's educated appreciation of jazz, her job as a social worker for the county, and her husband, Steve, who worked as an electrician at Fernwood. Mandy was very bright and quite sweet, but though she spoke highly of her husband, it was clear to me that what she was expressing when she spoke of him was more of a detached fondness than love or passion. I left that night when she did, and walked her to her car before innocently kissing her on the cheek. "You're not in love with your husband, are you?"

"Steve is a wonderful man."

"I'm sure he is," I said, smiling. "Goodnight"

I had a hopeful feeling I would be seeing her again.

Morey Amsterdam, who to the best of my knowledge hadn't worked since the original *Dick Van Dyke Show*, came and went, Pat Cooper did a Saturday night show, and we played behind more *Aces* and *Lads* than you can shake a stick at. Lionel Hampton's band played a two-hour show, Buddy Rich appeared with his band of battered and abused young musicians, "*Tee and Company*" accompanied an aging Eartha Kitt, the *original* "Cat Woman," and I invited Mandy and Susan to one of my brother's concerts at Carnegie Hall. My sinister hope was that either they would both come along (and the three of us would have sex after the concert), or Mandy would be the only one to go (and I could then pursue her in a controlled environment).

During the ninety-minute drive to New York, my more realistic hopes satisfied, Mandy and I talked and laughed and quickly relaxed with one another. Mandy confessed that she hadn't liked me at all the first night we met, and I told her that she was probably in good company. Then she explained that her feelings had changed the night we all went to Susan's house, that she had decided then that I was a decent, and very appealing guy. Sometimes, it seems, first impressions should be trusted.

As we walked the streets of New York City in the hours before the concert, I took Mandy's hand, ostensibly to keep her from getting lost in the crowd. Jackets were required at The Aegean Sea Fare, just one of New York's many inexplicably reputable restaurants, and so I was asked by the Maitre' D, who I spied minutes later furtively picking his nose, not to remove my heavy leather jacket. The place looked nice enough, but served along with the overdone, allegedly fresh seafood we'd ordered from a twitching waiter were two identical piles of suspiciously familiar looking french fries—about the same size, shape, and quantity we might have obtained for thirty-nine cents if we'd gone across the street to McDonald's and asked for a small order of salty, greasy fries. Hmm. It was at that point that I finally removed my jacket, hoping for an opportunity to verbally assault the vile, fast-food-french-fry-serving, jacket-rule-enforcing, nose-picking, hyphen-inspiring weasel. He wisely left me alone. Oh well.

Later that night, as we sat in the concert hall waiting for the performance to begin, a small elderly man shyly approached us. He leaned over and asked, "Do you know who I am?"

"No," I said uncomfortably, not completely certain that he was directing his peculiar question toward me.

"I'm your father."

Do I know how to impress a woman, or what?

I hadn't seen my father for probably twenty years, and as strange as I know this sounds, the pallid, cavernous face that loomed over us was not at all familiar to me. But despite the discomfort that followed that brief, awkward encounter, the music that night was excellent, and during the two-hour concert there was further handholding, this time without even the pretense of the unimaginative but effective justification I'd earlier employed.

On the way home Mandy and I stopped at a quiet bar in New Jersey to talk and, I suppose, to delay our inevitable separation. After sitting there for about twenty minutes, circumnavigating what we were by that time both thinking and feeling, we resumed our drive. We stopped a for second time at The Deerhead Inn in Delaware Water Gap, where we had a second and probably a third drink before reluctantly yielding to our shared fate. It was in my pick-up truck in the dark parking lot outside the bar that, with her full cooperation, I first kissed and gently molested Mandy before delivering her back home to her trusting husband. Mandy told me the following day on the telephone that she nearly threw up when she got home—not, by the way, because I was so utterly revolting, but because of what our reckless moment might mean to her otherwise well-ordered life.

And she was right to worry. What a horrible mess we were about to make.

30

Damage

Mandy and I met in parking lots, out of town restaurants, and soon at my little basement apartment. Sometimes she would come to Fernwood, where we would sit at the bar on my breaks talking and acting like distant friends. On occasion she would invent excuses for staying out late, or, once or twice, all night. We carried on for quite a while before anyone who cared was aware of what was happening. Of course I had done all of this before, but always with the knowledge that I would be leaving the scene of the crime before it became too treacherous, always with the imminent comfort and hypothetical safety of distance.

And although I was certainly learning to care for Mandy, I surreptitiously continued my other sporadic extracurricular activities. I was still not able or willing to give myself fully, and exclusively, to one woman, though I think I might have tried for a minute or two. In any case, there was a shit-load of lying going on. Mandy was bright and pretty, but I was unable—perhaps because of my past pain or maybe because I was simply changing—to envelope myself in her in the way that I had, at least for a time, with a number of hapless women before her. And although what I was doing was no different in many ways from what I had done so many times before, looking back on it now, writing about it, it has a different feeling. Maybe it's because I know how much pain eventually came of that relationship, how much harm I feel I did, or maybe it is because I'm still not certain I was *ever* really honest with her. Perhaps it's just that it's more recent, that the wounds are fresher.

Nevertheless, our relationship grew more serious, for her at least, and soon she was speaking about leaving her husband. So my days were spent practicing obsessively, and my nights playing and flirting and worrying about the future, about what would become of me, and what would be expected of me if and when Mandy and Steve were divorced.

And while I was trying frantically to squeeze through life's loopholes and to construct my own, Tee's drinking was becoming even more of a problem. It took a long time for his wife, Donna, to recognize how serious it was, but when she finally did she became almost fittingly terrified. And although she was confused and uncertain how to react, Donna loved Tee and wanted to make their relationship work. She wanted to help him. And so did I.

Tee behaved in the way that so many people do when an addiction becomes apparent to those around them. I'm sure that a part of him recognized the problem, but the rest of him, *most* of him, was fighting hard to ignore the evidence and emphatically deny the facts to himself and everyone else. The addict in him was doing everything in its power to enable him to continue drinking. And it was a formidable force.

When he became aware that I was monitoring his drinking at the bar, he went out between sets to the bottle or bottles he kept in his car. At home he would start his morning with half a glass of orange juice and then find a reason to go to the garage, where he filled the remainder of the glass with vodka or gin. He was drunk before noon and for the entire day and night. He lied, he sneaked, he may have stolen; he did whatever was necessary to enable him to continue his uncontrollable self-destructive behavior. He did, in short, what addicts do.

And Donna and I did exactly what people who care about addicts do. We held him up when we probably should have let him fall, we covered for him and watched over him, and for a time we did everything possible to make certain he stayed out of the gutter. We couldn't help it either, of course. We didn't understand that the only chance he had was to land with an agonizing thud in the dirtiest, ugliest gutter he could find, and then to realize, if he was alive and if he still could, where he was and how he got there. And he might have gotten there sooner if not for his marriage into the family that owned the resort. He was now raising the grandchildren Bob had come to love. Firing him would have meant hardship and embarrassment for those children.

So…

Every night when I arrived at work I counted the change on the bar in front of him to see how many drinks he'd already consumed, and on the breaks I continued to monitor him. Sometimes on the way home I noticed his car hidden in a corner of the parking lot of the nearest roadside bar, and I became enraged. It still amazes me how far-reaching the peripheral effects of his behavior were. And I am not blaming him for *my* reactions; I am simply noting the connection. Waves move in all direction, unconcerned.

I think, I hope that I was a good friend to Tee. I know that as angry as I often became, I tried hard to be. My own issues were coming to the surface and clouding my vision, but still, my motivation, my *major* motivation was to keep this decent, troubled man from crumbling.

In time Steve and Mandy were divorced. She rented a one-bedroom apartment in town, leaving him the house, the furniture, and virtually everything but their burgundy Pontiac Sunbird—for which she was still paying. Meanwhile, I, for all the obvious reasons, maintained my own country hideaway, keeping my options open, doing the dance that by that time I knew so very well. Mandy's education and experience with social work, in addition to her own history with an alcoholic father, were helpful to me as well as to Tee and his family. She was always supportive and more than willing to offer assistance or advice. She lovingly kept me from becoming too caught up, or at least alerted me when I was in the process of doing so. She recommended local resources and made the necessary contacts. Mandy had a strong social conscience and a sincere concern for the welfare of those less fortunate or more confused than her. She was, in my opinion, and probably still is, a good person, but although she now lives only five blocks away from me, and has for almost two years, we never speak. And I guess I don't blame her. But it is still sad.

31

Everybody Sing

Rudiments are, to a drummer, what scales are to pianists and saxophonists and violinists and almost everyone else who plays or practices a musical instrument. Metronomes are, to a drummer, what traffic cops are to nervous teenage drivers. And it wasn't only rudiments and metronomes that I had to contend with; there were the independent coordination exercises, the rhythms I'd stolen from one drummer or another, the foot exercises, the reading exercises, and even the occasional, often futile attempts at creativity. So the long days of practicing in my little cocoon crawled painfully by, broken up by meals (mostly frozen lunches and dinners), and grooming (mostly showering and shaving), and housework (mostly vacuuming and dusting), and laundry (mostly socks and underwear), and telephone calls (mostly annoying), and random erections (mostly self-induced and self-fulfilled), and tanning on the roof with a book and a flyswatter, and *The Fugitive* and *The Rockford Files*, and thoughts of girls and women, and playing with my other toys, and thoughts of girls and women playing with my toys, and finally preparing for work. Nevertheless, I spent an impressive amount of time practicing, and given that, I am surprised that my improvement wasn't swifter or more dramatic than it was. Maybe my heart just wasn't fully in it, or maybe it was just that I wasn't focused, that most of my mind was elsewhere. Although I did improve, I never did become the great drummer I wanted to be.

The "talent" shows:

When democracy works it can be a beautiful thing, but when it fails, as in the case of the talent shows, wherein anyone, no matter what his or her level of shame resistance, can share a public stage with four reasonably proficient musicians and make a mockery of melody, rhythm, and everything else we, in the music industry, hold sacred, it must be acknowledged that not all men, or women, or even little boys and girls are created equal. And yet there apparently exists in the tiny brains of most humans and sub-humans a cruel and heartless gene that tells them, with vicious intent, that they can sing or dance or tell jokes or play drums, guitar, piano, accordion (God save us), or the trombone they just *happened* to have packed for their weekend in the Poconos. In short, anything you can imagine any aspiring fireman from Queens named Vinnie, who never *was* quite right in the head, if you asked the neighbor's dog, trying to do.

And every annoying little girl under the age of fourteen *had* to sing that fucking atrocious song from Annie. "Tomorrow, tomorrow, I love ya…" *Launch the torpedoes. Fire at will.* And every hairy twit Staten Island appliance repairman with a regulation pocket protector simply had to sing that other horrible fucking song. "Stawt spread'n du news, Ahm leavin' tudday." *Not soon enough, buttmunch.* Sometimes they actually brought their own sheet music. Were they really having fun?

At some point the resort's management realized, to our chagrin, that on the nights of the talent shows we were often packing up by ten o'clock while receiving what they considered to be full pay for the evening. It was then that they decided to allow the employees to join in the festivities in order to increase the duration of the excruciating exercise. Now, in addition to the increasingly irritating customers, we had to deal with every waiter and waitress and busboy and desk clerk and dishwasher and chef and Maitre' D and security guard and chambermaid and bartender and lifeguard who believed that it couldn't be *that* difficult to get up on stage in front of a stunned and often far too forgiving audience and make a complete ass of yourself.

I don't believe I will ever understand why nearly everyone thinks he or she can sing, dance, play an instrument, or tell jokes. It is a disease that can afflict anyone at any time; no one is immune. And if it were only themselves they were embarrassing it might be easier to take, but they always seem to take others with them on their way down. Are they deaf, I would ask myself, or just stupid? Or are they deaf and stupid? Are they unable to see or hear the difference, or is it just the total absence of shame? Or could it be that I am just a little angry?

32

A Bunch of Drunks

I don't know when it was that I began to truly care about the music, or when I first realized that I wanted so very much to be better than pretty good, but it happened—it sneaked up on me. Part of it, I suppose, was another function of my competitive nature and my needy ego, but there was also a potent though muted passion for the music, and a surprisingly strong sense of what was good and what was not. I was also gradually becoming aware that I might live past thirty, which theoretically meant I would need to make a living—an actual adult living. So I began to recognize the desire for something positive in my future, and I found myself wanting, despite my sense that I didn't deserve it, to feel pride and satisfaction. I had no idea, at the time, how much I was asking, or how much work and disappointment was still ahead.

It is difficult indeed to alter your lifelong programming, and I was hard-wired early on for disappointment, dissatisfaction, depression, and, at best, accidental limited success. The concepts of happiness and fulfillment were foreign to me, and far beyond my comprehension. I had satisfied the basic needs of my suffering ego for so many years through the interest of women and the responses I seemed to evoke. I'd established my value in their writhing, in their passionate moans and breathy sighs. And because that feeling, so dishonestly attained, never lasts, I had to repeat myself, jumping swiftly from one meaningless victory to the next, in a futile search for some elusive permanent support. This was all I knew.

And I am not making excuses; I was who I was, maybe who I had to be.

I watched as Tee and Gerry fed off of each other's worst behavior, drifting farther and farther from the world around them. Gerry, who bore a striking resemblance to Icabod Crane, was sitting down now during the shows, probably to avoid tipping over. And as his grasp on reality diminished, his bass playing grew louder and more offensive. He was no longer shy about his epic incompetence. In fact, one wonderful, unforgettable night, in the middle of a quiet ballad during Julie's show, I watched with a combination of horror and blithe amusement as Gerry teetered in his chair for a minute before toppling slowly off the stage. There was a dull thud and the resonant, boisterous twang of four open strings. I glared down at him as he tried clumsily to recover. "Just stay where you are," I said. "It's sounding better already." I believe his response was, "Huh? Huh? Wha?" And I'm not certain Tee even noticed.

Meanwhile, Billy was slurring his words, weaving and slobbering on stage, breathing toxic fumes into the bewildered little faces of the sweet children who performed in the talent shows. I told him more than once, covering the microphone so the entire audience wouldn't hear the angry admonition, to get off the fucking stage. Nelson Sardelli, one of the weekend performers, ordered Tee to sit down so I could conduct his show, and Mark, who was always, always late, was also, at this point, usually stoned (although I must admit that regardless of his condition, and in spite of some seed of innate talent, his playing was consistent in its mediocrity). There were only a few rare occasions when drugs or alcohol made Mark's thumping even less refined than when he was in his normal semiconscious state. Finally, when her in-laws threatened to fire the band because of her husband's unrestrained drinking, Donna's long warm-up to panic reached a climax.

I had begun to take all of this very personally. It mattered now, for some reason, how we sounded, how the music felt, and how people received us. I was angry with all of them, and frustrated at myself for remaining where it was safe, though increasingly uncomfortable.

I learned to love Mandy, but at such a distance that she could never really sense it, and with such reservations that it was, for both of us, insubstantial and virtually irrelevant. There was no promise in my love, no security. And so, although I did love her and respect her and like her so very much, like money in an account you don't know you have, money you will never see, it wasn't of much practical use to either of us.

I had a few nights with Karen, which were always enjoyable now that we weren't dating, and several one-night stands with a variety of young unfortunates. And after trying everything else, including a pill that promised to make him violently ill if he drank, and even the dramatic step of cutting back to only two bottles of Seagram's a day, Tee, with the encouragement of his friends and family, finally checked in to an alcohol rehabilitation center.

So...

While Tee was being looked after by the trained professionals, I was left in charge of the band, which meant, for me at least, that things went more smoothly than they had for quite a while. I did my best to keep Gerry and Mark under control, and to keep the owners, who had no clue what they wanted or needed, happy. I made certain, at the very least, that we performed our duties and went on stage when we were supposed to. And though there was some initial resistance to my leadership, I believe that, for the most part, we were all a little more secure, a little more relaxed during my temporary reign.

Then...

One evening when I arrived at the resort I noticed several new faces and the mysterious absence of a number of regular employees. There was a silent tension, which remained unexplained until very late that night, when I learned that a majority of the resort staff, including the Maitre D', several bartenders and most of the waiters and waitresses, had been involved in an organized scheme to rob the place blind. I will only say that I was shocked to learn of some of the people involved—I'd slept with several of them. I was, though I probably should not have been, stunned and a little disturbed. There was still a hint of foolish innocence left in me. But that was a long time ago.

33

The Child of Love

Mandy was always supportive. She was understanding of any pain or difficulty I experienced, as long as it had no direct negative impact on her. And I suppose that is normal and reasonable. She knew I was unhappy and she did her best to help me deal with my family relationships, and the absences thereof. It was with her support and encouragement that I finally decided to visit the unfamiliar man who'd introduced himself as my father on our first awkward date.

Off and on throughout my life my father had made mild, unenthu-siastic (as in pathetic) efforts to renew contact with me (not that we'd ever really had any contact worth noting). But even after all my broth-ers had established their own limited adult relationships with him, I was not convinced of the value of such a thing. It seemed obvious to me that, since I had survived so many years without a father, I didn't need one, and that all we had in common anyway was that I was the product of a brief sexual encounter (a very brief and tedious encounter according to my mother, who never had the good taste to keep any-thing that might reflect poorly on my father to herself) between my mother and him. It's great to be the child of love, the product of a happy home. Nevertheless, as I became more and more aware of the depression that had most likely been skulking inside me for most of my life, and the limitations of my relationship with my mother and my four brothers, I decided to develop my own impression of the still mys-terious man my mother seemed to hate so fervently. Though she expressed her hatred very convincingly, she would never admit that she felt anything but sympathy for him. If you create your own world, anything can be true. If you believe you can fly, you'll land with a smile—and a splatter. "Look at me; I can f…" *Splat*.

My father, I learned, is a soft spoken and terminally passionless man; he probably is, and most likely has been for a long time, very depressed. He seemed to me a decent person, but someone with whom I had nothing at all in common, and with whom I would have no desire to form a relationship if not for the genetic link we happened to share. Nonetheless, despite my pessimistic view of the prospect of getting to know him, I resolved, with hopes, I suppose, of learning something about my family and myself, to make a cautious limited investment of time and emotion. And true to form I had the lowest expectations possible, in spite of the latent eager need even I didn't realize was subsisting quietly within me.

My father spent most of our first awkward meeting in his downtown office in Allentown trying to convince me that he was not the evil person he was certain I had been told he was. He was careful not to attack my mother directly, but he did express his firm belief that *he* was the victim, and that much of the information he assumed I received, was, at best, confused—which it may well have been. He assured me that his discharge from the Army had been an honorable one, despite what our mother might have said to the contrary. And I assured him that it was completely irrelevant to me. I couldn't understand how anyone could survive an experience like the one I imagined he'd had in the military during World War II without sustaining some psychological damage. A dishonorable discharge was, to me, just a slight burning sensation and a sticky green stain in your underwear. After that visit I felt no strong compulsion to see him again, but I had started something and I knew that I had an unspoken responsibility to continue it if I could.

Meanwhile, back at Fernwood, huge changes were taking place. Vince, the ancient guitar player and singer, retired, Bob Arnt found another girlfriend, putting Julie's job in jeopardy (oh well), and finally, after a short, futile battle with lung cancer, Ragtime Charlie Young left us for that great piano bar in the sky. I'll take hell, not that I've been offered a choice. Tee emerged from the rehab, sober, for the moment, and thinner and paler, but otherwise relatively unchanged. And soon the resort began its search for a replacement for Charlie.

I've never really understood the concept of non-stop "entertainment," the idea that if the mindless, sometimes melodyless noise stops, the discontented audience will flee en masse. But it wasn't up to me. So we had to suffer through an endless array of singles, duos, and trios, anxious to assault us all with shameless displays of hyperactive incompetence. Maybe it isn't so surprising that Tee soon began to drink again.

There was a portly accountant type who sang along melodramatically—coming really close to the notes for which I assumed he was aiming—with poorly pre-recorded tapes that lacked only a vocal track, and there was a Jamaican organ player who sang and played every song, regardless of how it was intended to be played, in the same key, the same time signature, and at the same tempo as the one that had preceded it, with a cheap, annoying drum machine repeating itself incessantly as he segued from one bizarre tender reggae love ballad to another. "*Some-where*, chunka, *overda' rainbow. Mon*, chunka, *dots*, chunka, *high*." As with the "talent shows" there was, and probably still is, an inexhaustible supply of people who, despite the substantial limits of their ability, were perfectly comfortable, even jubilant, displaying publicly that which they could do no better than almost anyone who'd suffered through a few piano, guitar, or cassette player lessons. And it seemed as though no one could tell the difference, which didn't say much for our audience. If you could buy, rent, or borrow a drum machine, a guitar, or a Casio keyboard, you could find work. At Fernwood. If only I could have found a way to blame my parents for that…

34

Europe on 45 Drinks a Day

Shortly after my reunion with my father, I took ten days of my very first, much needed, two-week paid vacation ever, to visit my brother Christopher in Europe. Chris and I had been in sporadic contact during the years that he'd been living in Germany, and he'd been expressing more and more fervently his frustration with his family's apparent lack of interest in his life there. So it was with a combination of guilt and excited anticipation that I flew, by way of Reykjavik, Iceland, with two cameras, four lenses, and thirty rolls of film, to Luxembourg.

After breezing through customs at the airport, I picked up the tiny red tin box with wheels I had reserved prior to my departure, loaded my luggage into the "car," and putted off in what I hoped was the general direction of Oldenburg, Germany, where Christopher was living and working as a musician, teacher, and militant communist. I took my time driving, both because I wanted to see the countryside, and because I was always completely lost, and, with the language barrier, often unable to ask for help, or to understand the answer when I did.

And it was a beautiful and exciting two-day expedition, first through a few colorful back roads, and then on the runway known as the Autobahn, where if you are brave enough or foolish enough to allow the speedometer to dip even a millimeter below one hundred fifty kilometers an hour (which, translated to miles per hour, is approximately too fucking fast), you are immediately run off the bustling flight path. They say there is only one kind of accident on the Autobahn: fatal. It is easy to believe. And what is truly unnerving is that while you're zipping along trying to decipher the few road signs as they pass in an unpronounceable blur and staying just ahead of the air traffic, a low roar approaches from behind you, headlights flash like strobes, and some ne'er-do-well in a Ferrari Red Ferrari careens around you so fast the heat from the turbo chargers singes your eyebrows into a permanent expression of astonishment.

Anyway...

Christopher was ready for me. On the day of my arrival there was a welcoming party that included table tennis, a barbeque, laughter, heavy drinking, and even a couple of fetching young frauleins. We had a great time that day. We played several dozen games of Ping-Pong, drank boatloads of beer, and I chose my next victim, Birgitta, pronounced, *beer-guitar*. She was cute, she spoke no English, and she was...fifteen (which, translated to American schoolgirl years, is approximately thirty-five and married). In New York, had I been interested, it probably would have cost me a hundred dollars to spend the night with a fifteen year old who spoke no English, and I can't imagine that either of us would have enjoyed it very much.

Chris and I spent the days together traveling and laughing and acting almost like brothers, and in the evenings his girlfriend would come over with her little sister, Beer-guitar, and the four of us would attempt to communicate before finally going to our separate corners, where we would happily yield to the impossibility of meaningful verbal communication. And after several fun and alcohol filled days and nights with Christopher and his friends I finally went off alone, in eager search of the Europe I'd never seen.

I drove south with no clear goal, attempting again to enjoy the racing scenery, and soon I found myself lost in Munich, where I did almost nothing for a day or two before heading into the stunning Austrian Alps. And in the Alps I got lost once more.

Although I have lived most of my long and, I hope, interesting life, without any apparent goal to guide me, I've never been particularly comfortable driving without one. There is no way to chart your progress, and you are constantly called upon to make difficult and potentially significant decisions. I guess the major difference is that when driving, I generally hope or expect to *eventually* get to some specific place at some approximate time, whereas in life, I never want to end up where I know I eventually must, and I certainly have no time frame that I'm aware of, which means that I can put off any important or difficult decisions indefinitely. How strange.

Although I didn't completely miss the beauty of the verdant Austrian countryside, I was not able to relax and enjoy the scenery or the people nearly as much as I probably should have, as much as I might have had I been someone other than me. Nonetheless, I drove along unmarked winding roads traversing the towering mountains through late afternoon. At dark I stopped at a small hotel nestled at the edge of the forest on a lovely road I'm sadly certain I could never find again. In the warm, cozy lobby, I was greeted by a little round woman with an impressive mustache. She spoke no English, and I, an inveterate monoglot, spoke *only* English and a bizarre sign language that to my surprise and embarrassment I was inventing on the spot. Consequently it took a while for me to get my message across, but she eventually made the assumption that I wanted either dinner or a room. I wanted both.

My room was gorgeous, with a brobdingnagian bed, a luxurious bathtub the size of Maine, and a massive pair of sliding glass doors, which I would learn the following morning opened onto an incredible view of a dark, impenetrable forest overshadowed by snowcapped mountains adorned in misty gray scarves. The suite cost me approximately eleven dollars, and the exceptional meal, served by a slightly plump, strangely familiar girl with an impending mustache, cost only a couple dollars more and was nearly as large as the room. I would go back there someday if I had any idea where it was.

The following day, aware that my time in Europe was running out, I left early for Heidelberg, with vague hopes that my night in Austria would somehow help me in my own efforts to grow more substantial facial hair. I actually used a map, this time, to find my way.

It was late afternoon when I found comfortable if unremarkable lodging in Heidelberg, and I took my time settling in before setting out in search of food and fun. I have no recollection of my dinner that evening, but I do recall roaming around the ancient city afterwards, admiring the architecture and the beautiful women as I strolled past quaint shops and beautiful antique churches. And I remember the familiar sense of desperation and desire I felt as I walked the streets. I was hoping for a miracle.

I wandered for quite a while before deciding it was time to find something else to do. Finally, in carnal desperation, I approached a tall, radiant woman with blond hair, lovely long legs, and a munificently short skirt.

"Do you speak English?" I blubbered, trying not to seem too threatening while I assessed her hilly northern regions.

"Yes, I do." She said, and smiled.

"Do you know if there are any jazz clubs in Heidelberg?"

"Oh, you like *jazz*?"

My heart was racing and my penis was beginning to stir, sifting through the dusty contents of my pockets. "Yes, uh…do you?"

"No, not really so much," she said with a pleasant accent, and I felt the terrible pain of disappointment in my withering groin. "But there is one club called Cave 54 a couple of blocks away."

"Well, um, okay, um thank you. Um." I responded cleverly.

I went alone to Cave 54, laughing to myself about the name of the place, hoping I would find that for which I was constantly searching. I didn't have high hopes for the music, but that was, as always, only a secondary consideration.

It was early when I arrived at the dark, truly cave-like nightclub, and so I sat at the bar drinking a glass of wine, assessing the situation as people filtered in and the band set up. The designers of this club had clearly had an idea, a plan. The problem was that they had followed it. First, they blatantly borrowed the "54" from the then famous Studio 54 in New York City—not a place famous for its great jazz, by the way—and then, adding poor taste to silliness, they used low light, dull gray paint, wire mesh, and papier mâché to create an environment visually similar to the one that prehistoric man wisely escaped at his first opportunity. My expectations were diminishing. And then, finally, the band began to play. And they were most impressive.

I was still at the bar after the first set, when the pianist and bass player sat down near me. They ordered their drinks and I turned to speak to them.

"You guys sound great."

"Thanks, are you from the U.S.?"

"Yeah, I'm here on vacation."

"Are you a musician?" the pianist asked, moving closer.

"Yeah, actually I play drums."

"Hey, you know who you look like?"

And before I could respond the bass player noticed it too. "Yeah, he looks like Keith Jarrett."

"He's my brother," I confessed.

Well, these friendly, gifted guys, whose names I wish I could recall, were in awe, not of me of course, but of the fact that they were this close to Keith Jarrett's younger brother. But once they got beyond the initial shock, they were very sweet and happy to get to know who I was. They were excellent musicians and very nice people.

I remained for their second set, and afterwards they all came over again to talk and laugh and drink, and then to ask me if I would like to play a couple tunes with them. I was nervous and excited and becoming inebriated, but I played at least one entire set with them. And though the four of us consumed enormous quantities of wine and liquor before, during, and after playing, we played surprisingly well and laughed our asses off until the club was otherwise empty and the sun was beginning to faintly tint the distant dark horizon.

It was a memorable night in many ways, not the least of which was that I'd played good music with good musicians and had not, to the best of my knowledge, embarrassed myself. They were impressed. The only problem was that when I walked out into the cool early morning air I discovered that I was horrifically drunk and totally lost. I can't be certain of course, but I probably stumbled around the city for hours before finally finding, completely by lucky accident, the hotel where I would vomit my beleaguered guts out until noon.

After I'd purged through every available orifice all solids, liquids, and even a couple things that looked an awful lot like vital organs, the room smelled like a dumpster and so did I. But this was my final full day in Europe, and so I had to drive, despite the terrible pounding in my spinning head and the uneasy turning of the remains of my tortured stomach, to Luxembourg, from where I would be parting, if I survived, early the following morning.

Early that evening I checked in to a hotel near the airport. In a nearby restaurant I ordered what was charitably described as a slice of pizza and what they repeatedly swore, despite my expressions of fear and incredulity, was a Coke. I did not believe them then and I certainly don't believe them now. It was the worst alleged pizza I've ever attempted to eat, and the "Coke" tasted like industrial waste, but lacked the thirst quenching properties. And the combination of this meal and my self-induced super sensitivity led to another long, difficult night, and, I suspect, the loss of a few other previously internal organs.

Things at home hadn't changed much in my absence, but I came back sporting, along with the remains of my hangover, a more positive sense of myself as a musician, and just a subtle hint of enthusiasm and ambition. While easily falling back into my old routine, I actually allowed myself to feel better...for a time.

35

Armed and Dangerous

I t is so odd how we get where we do, coming from where we have. For me it began with a family already deeply immersed in music by the time I was born. One brother was so exceptionally talented that no one ever thought to doubt his imminent success, and another exhibited early hints of a similar potential. By the time I was in my teens Keith had achieved more than many gifted people do in their long lifetimes; he had developed a name and a following, and though he probably had his own doubts, his future was secure. It was only natural then that each of my parents' sons would at least toy with the idea of learning to play a musical instrument.

For me it was never, it could never be the passion it seemed to be for Keith. I did it, I suppose, because of my relatively minor natural ability, and because it was something to do—and perhaps because it was expected. Indifferently, I took piano lessons when I was five or six years old, a few violin lessons a year or two later, and then, in my very early teens, I suffered through several bitterly discouraging saxophone lessons. *Honk, squeak.* There were all sorts of instruments in our home, but it wasn't until I finally found myself sitting behind Christopher's drum set, that I had the realization that *this* was an instrument I could probably play very poorly without taking a single lesson. And I was right. So at the age of fifteen, having illegally dropped out of high school a couple years earlier (with my mother's proud support), I found a drum teacher.

Jerry was a reasonably proficient jazz drummer who had finally found his true calling in getting stoned. He was a nice middle-aged man with a powerful addiction, a little barrel-chested guy with a funny miniature buzz-saw voice who did the best he could, given the condition of his ill-treated body and brain, to help me in my quest to pass the time painlessly. I was fond of Jerry, and knowing him was probably a very effective way to learn about some of the evils of excess, but I didn't learn a heck of a lot from him about playing drums. I, like so many other aspiring musicians, didn't want to have to actually study and practice—I wasn't *that* interested in music. It was while I was on the road with Fred Waring Jr., or shortly thereafter, that Jerry died of an overdose of whatever was available, leaving a young son and daughter behind.

But now, at the age of twenty-whatever, I found myself focusing more and more on the music. And I still don't know what motivated me, if it was a love of music, the dread of a barren future, or the need to prove something. Whatever my reason or reasons, I was now directing some portion of my obsession toward my musical skills and my career. It may even have been my pride, or hopes of meeting an entirely new category of women. It was probably all of that and much more. It was also probably a little late. And there were certain luxuries and obsessions, such as meaningless sex with a variety of partners, and true love, that I was still not willing to sacrifice for the music, or for anything else.

So I played around with the tall, handsome Maitre D's pretty new wife, Mary, and, after their separation, with the tall, handsome Maitre D's pretty new girlfriend, June, who screamed like an opera singer and was perfectly happy (for a while) sharing me surreptitiously with Mandy. I bought a bigger, better motorcycle, I practiced at least five days a week, and I watched as Tee's uncontrolled drinking increased yet again. And then I pissed a couple people off.

There was a dip-shit named Dip-Shit who used to sit at the Gaslight Bar with his nervous little dip-shit wife, Mrs. Dip-Shit, flashing hundred dollar bills and talking about how rich and tough he was. One night, during a ballad in our show, Dip-Shit decided it would be very clever to sneak up onto the stage and make even more of an ass out of himself than usual, and to a larger audience. Why do assholes feel the need to advertise? It isn't necessary; we can tell. Anyway, he proved his absolute idiocy by doing the ugly beginning of a drunken striptease, which upset Julie and at least confused the audience. So after the show I approached him to let him know how proud I was of him.

"Hi," I said, smiling as I gazed up into his empty, close-set, German shepherd eyes. "I just wanted to tell you," I paused, knowing he would be eagerly anticipating an expression of respect and admiration of his awfully darned shrewd display of unbridled wit and ingenuity, "that you have almost as much class as a sweat-sock." I turned and walked away, only gradually becoming aware of what I had said and the wide range of possible consequences. Maybe I ain't too smart neither.

The following evening I learned that the reason Dip-Shit had "temporarily" chosen not to shoot me in the face was that his wife had said, when learning of his intentions—and this, according to my sources, is an exact quote, "Awe, hon, you can't kill one of Tee's guys."

And…

A couple weeks later, as I prepared to pull away from the mailboxes in front of the Stroudsburg Post Office, a fucking slimeball named, I think, Roger "Slimeball" Kimball, who was temporarily employed laying carpet in a nearby office, turned—despite the presence of my shiny blue truck directly in his path—toward the parking lot. He crashed in to me, causing serious damage to my truck's right front quarter panel and bumper with his filthy white Dodge van. After we exchanged documents, I rushed across town to get an estimate, but when I came back to present him with the document I noticed a subtle change in his attitude. I believe his carefully chosen words were, "That ain't my prollum."

I learned in the days following that incident that the information with which Roger had so obligingly supplied me was not quite accurate. His registration was expired, his plates were illegal, and, despite what he had shown me, he was uninsured. When I tracked him down and called him to suggest that if he didn't pay me I would be forced to take legal action that might result in his having to pay, not only for the damage he'd done to my truck, but also the substantial fines he would likely incur for his other criminal behavior, he simply said that if I pursued this any further, he would murder me. My response? "Now I'm going to have to sue you for threatening my life too, you ignorant fuck-bubble©." I too *may* have had something of an attitude problem.

These two apparently unrelated incidents lead, at least in part, to a decision that was both out of character and potentially quite hazardous. I purchased, for several hundred dollars, a shiny new Ruger Security Six, a .357 Magnum with a shiny black six-inch barrel. This, for those of you who aren't well versed in weapon-speak, is a big and powerful revolver capable of causing injury, death, and even a really loud bang. Acquiring a license to buy a gun in Pennsylvania was frighteningly easy. But equally as frightening was the ease with which I obtained a permit to conceal the deadly weapon any damned place I pleased. This is not good, I am fairly certain. Would *you* let me carry a gun? The good news is that, despite rumors to the contrary, neither of these brainless, would-be thugs ever actually killed me, and that, despite a sometimes-dangerous temper, I never shot anyone.

Unfortunately, although *I* had years earlier given up the illusion that to be killed was somehow nobler than to defend yourself, Mandy was terribly disappointed and manifestly displeased with me. My decision to buy a gun would taint (or maybe correct) her peculiar view of me for a long time to come. And I really didn't like the idea very much either. It was just that I found it preferable to some of the options that were being so enthusiastically offered. Mandy, on the other hand, could neither forgive nor forget my decision. And although I eventually won my case against Roger Kimball in small claims court, he never paid me a penny. The fuck.

When I recall the timid child I was, how at age five and well beyond I would blush when my mother introduced me to some looming stranger, how my eyes would begin to water if he or she eyed me for too long or addressed me directly, how I seemed to shrink into myself until I nearly disappeared, and how I clung to that almost neurotic timidity even into my early teens, how I wept when a bug was swatted or an unwary squirrel pancaked under the tires of my mother's car, I am baffled by my dramatic transition to whatever it was I became. How do we get from there to here? How does a child so gentle, so painfully introverted and withdrawn become a raging, pistol-toting, priapic madman? In the end, like both of my motorcycles, I think I kept my gun just long enough, selling it to a gun shop before it got me into any serious trouble. These choices can quickly, easily alter a life, or take it. The threads upon which the mysterious stories of our lives hang are ever so delicate.

And…

Gerry's wife, who went by the stage name of Jody Ford, probably to avoid any association with her drunken dim galoot of a husband, would occasionally fill in for Julie when Julie wanted or needed a night off to swallow. Jody was not an absolutely terrible singer, though she was a singularly unpleasant person, and I would soon learn to loathe her. Nevertheless, when Julie, who had been gradually losing her voice and rapidly gaining enough mass to sustain her own murky atmosphere, was finally "let go" and we were asked to find a less expansive replacement, Jody seemed the unfortunate obvious choice.

Shortly after we hired Jody, Tee nearly died in the hospital. Trying hard to withdraw or escape, he suffered bizarre hallucinations as his body and his will seemed to whither. He'd been rushed to the emergency room one evening after the alcohol finally got the best of him, and when I went in to visit him, his wrists and ankles were strapped to the bed frame. He wriggled and complained and groaned while his mind traveled in and out of the fantasies it was creating, I assume, to dull the pain. He was thin and pale, somehow hollow. If he survived, it seemed clear, this would be his final chance.

I was a regular visitor in the hospital, and when he went off to the rehab I took leadership of the band for a second time, this time with the understanding that when Tee came out, whatever his condition and state of mind, he would not be coming back to work.

Things went smoothly enough until, several weeks into my new reign, I arranged a meeting with 'owner Bob' to request a raise to compensate me fairly (I thought) for my increased responsibilities, and small "cost of living" increases for the sidemen. I imagine Bob was already disenchanted with the band (what's the point of having an expensive, mediocre band if you're suddenly procuring your blowjobs elsewhere?). And I must admit he made a couple of valid points, such as the fact that we hadn't changed our repertoire for well over a year...or ever. But I was going to change that, I explained, and he would finally get his money's worth, by gum. He wasn't buying it. Oh well.

Nevertheless, given the paucity of career options, I remained at the resort for a while longer—long enough to hear the unsavory but probably accurate rumors about Jody's alleged late-night, parking lot oral activities with "owner Harvey," who, by the way, was about eighty years old and looked like a very old frog, but lacked the average frog's winning personality. And long enough to begin to feel myself becoming dangerously disgusted with the entire ridiculous place, as well as my own growing sense of stagnation and futility.

36

Yee-Ha

Corporeally, Mike Geradi was a monster, well over six feet tall and nearly as many around. In spite of his real estate statistics though, he was one of the few adult contestants in the Thursday night talent shows who had ever demonstrated even the slightest hint of talent (the truth is that several of the children were actually quite good). Mike was a reasonably mediocre bass player and a tolerable singer who had his own local quartet in Croton-on-the-Hudson, about an hour north of Manhattan, in New York State. Every year he would bring his poor, undoubtedly bored family to Fernwood, and every year he would play and sing with our band in the Thursday night talent shows, "*Celebrate good times, come on.*" Anyway, he seemed like a nice enough guy, and he didn't completely suck as a musician, so when he called to offer me a job playing with his band, deeply frustrated with the resort, and certain now that things weren't going to improve, I decided to quit Fernwood and join his band. Oops.

Mike's band wasn't terrible, but they were awfully close. Mike was the lead singer, an arrogant (without justification) late forties asshole named Steve Buttmunch, I believe, played guitar acceptably well, and Frank, who taught piano to unfortunate first and second graders, always just one simple lesson ahead of them (and trying very hard to hold his slim advantage), owned the keyboards. In addition to the problem of a total absence of inspiration, I found myself traveling almost two hours a night in each direction, except on those occasions when I chose to sleep or lay uncomfortably awake on one or another of the other band members' musty couches, in which case I would spend the following endless day in Croton-on-the-fucking-Hudson with nothing to do but read (with the fucking television and children screaming in the background) and wish I was anywhere else or that I hadn't sold my fucking gun.

Not surprisingly, Mandy resented my extended absences, I quickly learned to hate the traveling and the band, and soon enough everyone began to feel my unconcealed frustration. It was during my brief mistake with the duffers in Croton that I received the completely unexpected call from a gifted saxophonist named George Younger.

George was one of a surprising number of successful musicians who made their homes in the Pocono Mountains. I had, by coincidence, been playing after hours at the Deer Head Inn, the small jazz club outside of which I first kissed Mandy, one fateful night months earlier, when George and I met on stage. I was walking to my table at the end of the last set that night when George approached me to ask for my phone number. He explained that he was putting a band together and said that he would like me to consider playing drums with them. I knew who George was—I had seen and heard him playing around the area and was in awe of his substantial talent and his absolute comfort with his instruments—so his interest in me was a wonderful surprise. And although I certainly hadn't forgotten that encouraging conversation, I never really expected to hear from him again, so his call, during this terribly frustrating time, was most welcome.

He wanted to put a band together, he told me a second time, and then start playing, first, for some unexplained reason, in Atlantic City, and then around the world and beyond. There were no immediate bookings, but the long-term goal, as he explained it, was to record an album and do a concert tour, after which we would simply ride the inevitable wave to untold fortune and fame. The time frame was unclear, as were a number of other things, but still, this was as close to the dream that had been cautiously pushing its way toward my consciousness as I could ever have imagined coming. Although it was only a vague and distant possibility at this point, I could finally feel myself moving gradually toward something. I just couldn't be sure what it was, and it wasn't in my personality profile to become prematurely excited.

Also…

Working with Mandy as a social worker at the Monroe County mental health center at the same time was Mike Strunk, a very nice, fortyish guy, who, on most weekend evenings, put a cowboy hat over his cut-rate toupee' and played guitar in a country band called *Area Code 717*. When their bass player, Matty, thoughtlessly committed suicide in his garage, they found themselves in sudden urgent need of a replacement, and though I had never played bass or guitar before, my desperation to extricate myself immediately from the ugly situation in Croton was such that I asked Mandy to ask Mike if I could borrow a bass and come to a rehearsal to audition. It was an interesting moment in my career, and probably, in some way, a sign of my growing confidence. Or something. I had the inexplicable and totally unproven idea that I could somehow do this. I knew I had a good ear, and certainly a good enough sense of rhythm, and the rest, I believed, was mostly math, patterns, and manual dexterity.

Wayne, in whose basement that rehearsal was held, was the willowy lead vocalist and rhythm guitar player, Mike played lead guitar and did some background vocals, a postal servant named Matt played drums (and, I assume, made explosive devices), and Delroy Schneck, a big, mean looking part-time tractor-trailer driver with a wife named Aggie, played pedal steel. I was something of an outcast, and we all knew it.

So after brief, awkward introductions, Delroy looked at me with evident distaste and, as I plugged the borrowed bass into the borrowed amplifier, he said, in a thick Pennsylvania Dutch accent, "Okay now, key of 'C'."

"Um, no problem," I blubbered. "But…could somebody please point out exactly where that is on the bass?" I was ever so serious. Now where the hell did I put that silver shirt?

Most country music is not harmonically or rhythmically complex, and the bass parts seldom require enormous technical prowess (which is not to say that some country musicians aren't incredibly capable—indeed many of them are), so in many ways it was no surprise that I was able to start working with *Area Code 717* two weeks later, and to do a *reasonably* good job. On the other hand, I was proud of my ability to fit so apparently easily in to this surprisingly able group of musicians. When the band played well, the music, in spite of its simplicity, or maybe precisely because of it, felt as good as music can feel. Sometimes we played our asses off. And Wayne sang like an angel.

I have no wish to exaggerate the ease with which I learned this new instrument well enough to do a decent job; it took time and a fair amount of practice to get to the point where I dared to think of myself as a "country bass player." I understood my limitations, and I never called myself a bass player without being careful to insert the critical qualifier, "country." And maybe my accomplishment was not so remarkable after all. It is possible, I imagine, that any relatively bright, coordinated person with time, interest, practice, a little innate ability, and the proper tools could learn to perform quite competently a single complex surgical procedure. Of course that would not make him or her a doctor. And I wouldn't let the fucker near me with a scalpel.

In any case, playing with *Area Code 717* was often fun, and it was also interesting in so many ways. I was accepted into a culture very different from my own, and the experience widened my horizons and brought me a lot of joy. We played good music well without a lot of unnecessary angst; we laughed and drank beer, and, in spite of our stark differences, got along exceedingly well, playing in every dive, firehouse, and fairground for fifty miles in any direction. Yee-ha.

Meanwhile, George, who had been busy doing the mindless studio work that kept him comfortably supplied with the finest cocaine, engaged my friend, Eric Doney to play keyboards, and Tony Marino, whom I knew, but had never played with, to play bass. And then the long and daunting rehearsals finally began. I suppose there is always a balance of some kind, so maybe it makes sense that, given George's extraordinary technical prowess as a musician, he should be lacking in some of the more basic human skills. Nevertheless, it was frustrating to learn that in addition to his other significant limitations, George was not a great, not a good, or even a passable communicator. And he used an enormous quantity and variety of drugs to keep him from accidentally making any sense at all. Maybe nothing is easy, but sheesh.

In spite of the challenge of the rehearsals with George, and the possibilities suggested by them, I remained skeptical of my future as a musician, and so I continued searching for and often finding new women and girls with whom to satisfy the commanding needs of my greedy body and my increasingly ravenous ego. Even *I* wondered at times if my fierce desperation was more of an addiction than a desire, if there were deeper psychological issues at work than I had ever allowed myself to imagine, or than I could ever begin to understand. And of course Mandy sensed my distance, if not the specifics of my activities, and was disturbed and angered by my stubborn unwillingness to commit. And who can blame her? I suppose that, given my bizarre history, my own unhappiness, and the difficulties Mandy and I were experiencing, it was inevitable that I would eventually give in to her mandate that we go together to a therapist. Oh my.

37

A Real Live Mental Health Professional

My first experience in therapy was with an alleged therapist named Dick Milner. Make a note of that name. Now tear it up. Mandy had gone to "little Dick" years before, and, having felt fairly comfortable with him, she now wanted us to see him as a couple. And Dick did *every*thing wrong. He told bad jokes and took phone calls during our sessions; he took sides—or *hers* anyway—and entertained silly competitive arguments with *me* about issues that should never have arisen in the first place. He sat next to Mandy, completely inappropriately joining forces with her and against me. The fact is that he did not help us at all, and I spent our concluding session with him telling him what a poor job he'd been doing. It was the one time in my life that I felt absolutely certain I was getting my money's worth with a therapist.

"Dick," I said, as if referring to an unsavory body part, "this is going to be our last session with you, so I'd like to take a moment of the time for which you're overpaid to tell you why." I did not wait for his response.

"First of all, Dick, you spend an inordinate amount of time telling jokes while you are theoretically supposed to be listening to our thoughts and feelings. Even if your jokes were vaguely humorous, which, I assure you, they are not, that would be an unacceptable waste of *my* time and money."

"Well I can see that you are upset…"

"Dick?"

"Yes?"

"I am paying you fifty dollars for this forty-five minute session, so shut up and listen for a change. You might accidentally learn something. In addition to the 'jokes' there are the constant phone calls that you choose to take, despite the fact that you have both an answering machine and a receptionist."

"I think we can work some of this out, Grant."

"Well, the problem is that beyond all of that, you are completely incompetent and in way over your head. I think you should seriously consider other work, maybe manual labor of some kind, where there is no actual contact with actual humans. You don't know how to listen and you can't keep your own oversized ego from getting in the way. You sit and argue with me endlessly, as though we were little boys quarreling over a toy, as though the issues we are theoretically here to address have anything at all to do with you outside of the sad fact that you seem to have an unresolved crush on Mandy. You act as though you're in competition with me. If you have succeeded in doing anything, *Dick*, it has been to drive us more quickly apart. In short, *Dick*, you aren't particularly bright and you haven't got an objective bone in your brain."

There was a long, uncomfortable silence as Dick and Mandy processed my monologue. Mandy was angry and upset with me, and yet I still believe she knew that at least *some* of what I was saying was true. How could she not have known? She was staring at the carpet when Dick said, essentially, "I do *not* argue with you."

"Do *too*," I said in a child's voice, smiling sarcastically. Steam began to pour from the top of Mandy's head.

"Do you think there is anything we can do to make you change your mind?"

"Who is *we, Dick*?"

"Mandy and me, of course?"

"That's a revealing way to pose the question, isn't it? What *you* can do for me, *Dick*, is think about what I've said before you do serious harm to someone who's not bright enough to recognize your incompetence, like maybe a slug, or a stalk of broccoli. Start searching the want ads for something that requires no intellectual or communication skills—maybe, as an added bonus, your new coworkers will appreciate your lame fucking jokes."

It is amazing, given that first ugly experience with therapy, that I would ever try again.

What has ninety-seven legs and fourteen teeth? *Area Code 717's* audience. I didn't meet a hell of a lot of compelling women while on the country circuit. There were one or two of course. You can almost always find what you are looking for, especially if it isn't what you really want or need.

For instance...

I can recall an evening at Glenwood, another one of the local resorts, that was, for those few in need of further evidence, indicative of the blinding force of my predominant drive, or the feebleness of my anemic will, or something. There was in the audience that evening a fairly attractive, though by no means stunning young woman. Throughout the course of the evening she had been sending out the signals to which I had become so keenly attuned. But when at the end of the night it became apparent that if I stuck around I would probably get my pee-pee wet, I remembered that I hadn't driven. Mandy had dropped me off and Wayne was supposed to take me back to her place. Nevertheless, I soon decided, without any idea how I was going to travel the five miles back to Mandy's apartment and my vehicle, to let Wayne leave without me.

It was five o'clock in the morning when I finally found myself trudging the dark, mountainous five miles to Mandy's apartment. I stopped at every stream and puddle along the way to try to wash the telltale fragrance from my hands, face, and embattled nether-regions. And when I finally arrived, I slid quietly into her bed, and, laying face down in the pillows, buried my still redolent hands beneath me. I wasn't a very good person, and I was a terrible partner. Ask Mandy.

I guess I've always found the narrow line between guilt and the fear of exposure a little vague, which is to say that I've never been certain whether the discomfort I sometimes felt in the aftermath of some of my less laudable (or more horrendous) behavior was brought about by guilt, or by the fear of being discovered and the potential ugly consequences (castration, for example) of that discovery. But whatever it was that I felt, it was seldom if ever a compelling enough force to prevent me from behaving deplorably. And in the end, I experienced such an odd mix of emotions (including, I admit with shame, pride for my conquest and my apparent capacity to charm) that I was always a little off balance and edgy. And I'm not looking for sympathy—I have no sympathy for myself—I am just being truthful, comfortably after the fact, of course.

Area Code 717 was a good band, and they were good, decent, likeable people who had become my friends, but the work was sporadic and the pay mediocre, and this was not what I thought I wanted to do with my life and my theoretical talent. So when George Younger booked the band that he now called *Low Profile* at Caesars Resort Casino Hotel in Atlantic City, I was happy for the opportunity to move on. Sort of.

38

The Big Time, Finally...Almost

We had been rehearsing periodically and doing a little recording in New York, so we felt fairly well prepared, but, because Caesars' management had never before hired a jazz group to play in their lounge, there was one unfortunate stipulation to our employment there. We were to hire a female singer to "break things up and keep the audience interested." Of course, in a casino the audience is never really interested anyway; we could have been a group of completely unskilled bozos playing very poorly an ill-chosen selection of the worst submusic of the past and present and no one would ever have noticed, or cared. I guess what I'm saying is that we could have been Joe Travers and *Phase Phore.*

Playing with *Low Profile* in Atlantic City was not the rewarding experience I'd foolishly allowed myself to hope it might be; it may have been an educational experience but it was mostly frustrating and depressing. Eric's playing was conspicuously uninspired, Tony and I never really clicked in the way that, to be effective, a rhythm section must, and with the unappealing combination of the daily effects of his significant drug and alcohol abuse, and the silent and formidable rage we all felt seeping out of him, George kept the entire band in a constant state of awkward tension. And the singer George hired to comply with the resort's requirements, the daughter of a well-known old jazz musician whose identity I will, out of respect, conceal, was unexceptional in every way except for her own remarkable capacity for alcohol consumption. Nevertheless, at our best, which wasn't too bad, or at our worst, which wasn't so good, this band, if it belonged anywhere, did not belong in a Casino lounge in Atlantic Shitty. Oh yeah, I slept with the lovely and skilled but probably anorexic singer from the band with which we shared our dressing room. What choice did I have? After all, she was comely and willing.

I have no fondness for resorts, and no interest in gambling, but Atlantic City, where huge garish resorts tower haughtily over crumbling all-but-forgotten slums, was even more depressing than I'd expected. Take a large, firm turd—go ahead, that's it; now smother it with stale chocolate sprinkles, glitter, and a dab of whipped cream, no, Cool Whip; now dip it into a bowl of sandy Jell-O. Now try to eat the fucker. Go on. See? See?

The waitresses looked like (and may have been) hookers, and the customers were generally either rich, bored, and angry, or old, decrepit, and equally angry. And they all shared one common flaw: they'd voluntarily traveled to an Atlantic City casino to get away from the daily grind. It was as slimy and unappealing a group as you will find outside of any Queens bowling alley on any Friday night. They probably loved me too. I'm sure some of them were wonderful human beings. Maybe.

Of course I had some fun in Atlantic City. There were a few rare moments of musical pleasure scattered randomly between my eternal search and the frustrating rehearsals with a bandleader whose beleaguered brain seemed to be disintegrating, and whose passion was spent on getting very stoned and obsessively creating new and always more horrible concoctions with his brand new industrial juicer. "Hey, you've got to try this, man," he would enthuse, his bulging, red independent eyes spinning like those of a crazed cartoon hypnotist, "it's a combination of radishes, tree bark, squirrel chunks, lemur droppings, and mustard seed." Why is it that so many devout drug addicts are such great believers in the wonders of "natural" food? And what is *un*natural food? Anyway, Eric and I spent time hanging out at the beach, drinking wine, and laughing, and Mandy came to visit and check up on me once or twice. And the people who appeared to be in charge at the casino were, at best, incompetent, and at worst, hostile and aggressive. Maybe I should have applied for a management position.

Then…

One night, toward the end of our engagement at Caesars, I was on the sixth floor waiting for the elevator in my civilian attire, holding my white shirt and drumsticks in my hand. I had just come from the dressing room and was heading back to the bar for a drink.

"Hey you," a rude voice growled from down the hall.

I generally don't respond to such informal greetings from strangers, so I ignored him.

"Hey you," he barked again. "What are *you* doing up here?"

I turned slowly and saw the uniformed security guard plodding toward me, looking as threatening as his ignorance allowed.

"I'm waiting for the elevator."

"What are you doing on this floor?"

"Balancing."

"What?"

I looked up at him and smiled. "I'm in the band. We have a dressing room on this floor, which is something you'd probably be aware of if you'd paid attention in junior g-man class. See? This is my white shirt; these are my drumsticks."

"Look wise guy, you're no guest in this hotel," he said, and followed me into the crowded elevator.

"No shit," I said, while the other guests listened. "If I were a guest you would be guaranteed to lose you job when I report to management how fucking stupid and disrespectful you've been."

"That's it," he said sternly, "I'm taking you in."

He actually said that before pressing the button on his big black walkie-talkie and announcing, "Plotkin here, meet me in the lobby. Suspect in custody. Over."

When I stepped out of the elevator I didn't look back. I knew that if officer idiot put a hand on me I would punch the fucker in the head at least once before he figured out how to fire his weapon. For all I know he may have drawn a bead on me from behind, and then just had a brief, disorienting spell of sanity. Nevertheless, in a belated effort to be fair, I will admit the possibility that there had been a sudden upsurge in the incidence of violent white shirt thefts that week, and that Plotkin was just doing his job, "Ma'am."

After a discouraging month in the smoky casino—an atmosphere that could not have been less conducive to any kind of creativity—we headed home, without a plan for the future. I know *I* was disillusioned by the experience of working with George in Atlantic City, and I suspect everyone else was too—perhaps George more than anyone else. And although no one was quite ready to give up on the idea of the band, it had become quietly apparent that there was some serious rethinking to do. The music or the band or some other mysterious element had never come together the way it should have, the way it would *need* to for the music to matter, and we all suspected, based on the silent anger that George had, in those last few days, been so effectively expressing (it was the only thing George expressed effectively, though I'm still not certain he realized he was expressing it), that Eric's days with the organization were numbered, and that the numbers were in the single digits. And it was never really clear that Eric was the root of the band's weakness. But it was very clear that George had, in his building frustration, singled him out.

Upon my return to Pennsylvania, my friends in *Area Code 717*, who had been getting by with a series of temporary replacements, generously welcomed me back, with the understanding that I thought of myself more as a jazz drummer than a country bass player, and that working with George would always be my first priority. I kept busy practicing, fucking around, and making a meager living doing occasional weekend work as a country bass player, and soon George replaced Eric with another gifted keyboard player by the name of Peter Philips. George's latest plan was to do some local concerts, including the Delaware Water Gap jazz festival, where we could theoretically show off to the natives, and to continue preparing for the album we were all still hoping to record.

Some of the many rehearsals with *Low Profile* took place in a recording studio in New York, which was a fascinating and educational experience for me. I met and played with some of New York's finest studio musicians, and had the sometimes exciting, often disturbing, and occasionally bitterly painful opportunity to listen repeatedly to every mistake I made, every poor choice and insipid futile attempt at something sublime. Shiiiiiiiiiiiiiiit! Reality is over-rated. And if I wasn't such a good musician I might never have realized my considerable failings. Having a good ear is not always an asset, and good playing cannot be forced.

But I tried to learn from my errors, and to gain satisfaction and inspiration from the few rare moments when my various skills mysteriously conspired, despite my limitations, to create a phrase or chorus that would give me hope, and the even rarer moments when it all came together to create something like music. I practiced and played and listened and worried and hoped until finally deciding it was time to take a chance, that even if I wasn't quite ready (and I wasn't), I had to act as though I was. So it was that I decided to move to New York City, and to try to be a real musician, playing real music with other real musicians. Really.

39

The Other Newlywed Game

I'd met Chris Allen once or twice through my brother Scott, who I assume was casually pummeling her between more meaningful relationships. When I disclosed to Scott my plan to move to the big city he informed me that the young Rock drummer had just bought a house in Queens and was looking for a tenant to help offset her mortgage. Queens was by no means an ideal location, but the timing was perfect, so I moved in, with the understanding that we would try the arrangement for a while and see how it worked.

A decent, moderately talented, comely woman with a well-designed body, Chris was still somehow lacking in sex appeal. And despite her more positive qualities, she was neither a good roommate, nor, from the vantage point of this tenant, a good, or even reasonable landlady. The thermostat was locked at fifty degrees or below, and her dogs—one of them a bloodthirsty cur—left steaming heaps of shit on the living room floor whenever she was away for more than a couple hours, filling the frozen air with a horrible vomit-inducing stench that would inevitably force me out of my nearly comfortable cocoon under seventeen blankets on the second floor. And Chris was not particularly flexible or accommodating (she complained repeatedly about the electric bill after I bought a small space heater for my room so that I might stave off deadly hypothermia and frostbite).

But there *were* some positive aspects to this situation. Chris charitably allowed me to study the lessons her teacher was charging her for, which I did tirelessly. And through her connections she helped me secure work and even passed on to me some of the work—most of which was, regrettably, with Irish bands and cabaret singers—that she was unable or unwilling to do. I practiced literally from morning until night, significantly improving my technical skills, but making Chris crazy and myself a little dizzy in the process. Most nights, still possessed and obsessed after a day of unceasing practice, I would repeat complex polyrhythms on my chest with my gloved hands, counting in a misty gray whisper as I drifted again into frozen hibernation. Unfortunately, the work I found through Chris in addition to the sporadic work I continued to do with *Area Code 717* and George Younger was still not quite enough to sustain me in New York. Finally, in bitter desperation, I was forced to look for a real job.

I had been commuting to Pennsylvania most weekends, keeping Mandy, if not satisfied, then in a temporary state of frustrated acquiescence. But when I took a full-time job at a clothing store in Manhattan and began to work more regularly in and around the city on weekends, she applied additional pressure. She had wanted us to live together for a long time, but now she was becoming much more assertive, and I was scared to death.

Meanwhile, and no surprise to the careful reader, I was having an affair, this time with Leslie, the shiny new wife of Mandy's good friend, Dr. David Goldstein.

Although David lived with his new bride on Central Park West in Manhattan, he worked four or five days a week at a doctor's office in Pennsylvania. Until his marriage, Mandy and I had always assumed the soft-spoken, faintly effeminate physician was gay. I first met Leslie when I went horseback riding with Mandy and a group of her friends and colleagues from work. At the very beginning of the hour-long ride, a horse named Rex sunk his huge brown teeth into my left thigh, but despite my considerable discomfort and the rapidly growing and intensely colorful hematoma, I couldn't help noticing David's startlingly lovely, long-legged wife.

The next time we met was on an unprecedented ski trip Mandy and I took to Vermont with essentially the same group of people. Because she wasn't feeling well that week, Leslie spent most of the daytime hours quietly reading in her room. But from the first night, when we all went out for dinner and drinks, and she and I ended up off in our own private corner gabbing about music and art, I knew that, in spite of everything that was wrong with the situation, which was everything, I wanted her.

Leslie was tall and thin, and she spoke with a soft voice that was enhanced by an English accent. Adding to her appeal was an appreciation for jazz. Depending on who you were, and the mood she was in when you inquired, she was a sculptress, a writer, a dream interpreter, or a jewelry designer. And no matter who you were, she loved to drink wine. Though I knew she had only been married for a couple months, I had a vague, hopeful sense that she was flirting with me.

Everything that was going on in my mind during that trip was inappropriate, and completely, decadently selfish. I knew it then, and I certainly know it now. Nevertheless, I stayed up late in hopes that Leslie would appear, and when she was up and about I found lame excuses to be near her. How many glasses of water can you drink? I thought about her when I went to sleep, and I wakened with her image in the frosty mornings. Although nothing actually happened between us during that time in Vermont, the stage was set for the future, when I would be living in Queens, and she would be alone in her dark, lonely apartment on the Upper West Side, both of us lacking in a real social life and brought together enthusiastically by our respective mates. "I'm so glad you two get along," Mandy would say, pleased, at first, that we'd made friends. And David would meekly echo the thoughtful sentiment.

I remember quite clearly the first night Leslie and I got together. We'd arranged during a prolonged phone conversation earlier that week, to have dinner and drinks on an evening when she would otherwise have been alone. On the appointed evening I drove in from Queens to meet her at their apartment; I was already privately, anxiously planning my tender assault. We went to an Indian restaurant in her neighborhood, where we ate fifty or sixty different kinds of bread before ordering curried laughing lamb snouts and our first bottle of wine. After dinner, deep in intimate conversation, we continued to drink. It was toward the warm end of our second bottle of white wine that I shyly confessed to Leslie what I was feeling. And I meant everything I said that night. I truly *did* have a feeling for her that felt to me like more than distant fondness and prurient desire. And as we clenched each other's hands across the table, she confessed that she felt an attraction to me.

And so...

On the floor of their apartment that night, with Pat Metheny playing sixteenth note flourishes on their stereo, Leslie and I made love—anxious, voracious, forbidden, though very tender love—for the first time. I never got to know David very well, and although I know that this does not excuse my deplorable behavior, and does nothing to address the obvious issue of my infidelity to Mandy, I hold it out as a desperate attempt to suggest that there was some way in which the situation *could* have been more unforgivable than it already was, and that maybe, under those imaginary circumstances, I would have exercised some self-restraint. Hopefully, I'll never have to prove it.

And, in fact, it did get worse.

We continued seeing each other, sometimes making vain attempts to appear to control our passion, while at others easily, greedily giving in. And when, as occasionally happened, three or four of us got together, Leslie and I would furtively touch each other's hands or rub up against one another to feel the intoxicating warmth of the dangerous fire we had so carelessly ignited. Slaves to passion, or maybe just selfish and weak. Maybe just human. You decide. I would be too forgiving. Or too harsh.

It was well into my illicit "relationship" with Leslie that Mandy decided she was no longer willing to tolerate our separate living arrangement. And that is when I did what may have been the stupidest, most selfish thing I've done in my entire stupid, selfish life. Without divulging any of the ugly details to her, thank God, I admitted to

Mandy that I had been unfaithful. It was, in every way, a horrible thing to do. And I have no excuse. It was *not* better than lying about it. What would have been so *much* better, would have been to have the respect for her, and the strength of character to leave her.

The two reasons I used to convince myself that I had to tell her about my behavior could not have been more disparate. First, it was the right thing to do—the only fair thing in light of her plan to uproot herself, quit her job, and move into a city for which she had no particular fondness so that she could be with me. And second, it was the one thing I could do, in my epic cowardice, that might compel her to change her mind about living with me, and thereby save me the unpleasantness of eventually having to take upon myself the responsibility for that cruel initiative. What a confusion of emotion I felt, and how much more terrible it must have been for her, in love with a charming illusion, reliving, in some ways, her own angry mother's sad life. Fuck.

There was, of course, a lot I didn't tell her. I didn't tell her how many women I'd been with (after endless interrogation I told her there had been three others), or when it had all begun. I didn't tell her that I was sleeping with her friend, and I certainly didn't tell her about the night that Leslie and I had spent quietly groping one another on the now familiar living room floor while David slept soundly, unaware in the bedroom down the hall. But the most important thing I didn't tell her was that I wasn't certain I could ever change, or even certain that I really wanted to.

Because it isn't possible to say with any conviction what Mandy was feeling, I can only relate, with shame, what that time felt like from my perspective.

I guess I was in love with Mandy, and had been for a long time, but I was, or seemed to be, incapable of the kind of love that sustains itself and those fortunate enough to share it. I always wedged something or someone between us, maybe to protect myself, or maybe to protect her. Maybe just because I was greedy or incompetent or gutless. I was frightened of relinquishing my sense, however illusory, of freedom, and frightened too of limiting my options. At the same time I wanted to protect her from me, from the pain for which I felt, and often truly was, responsible. Despite my behavior, and the substantial effects thereof, I never wanted to hurt Mandy, and I hated myself for it when I did. And yet I did hurt her, repeatedly.

And...

As with so many things in life, Mandy's reaction, after the initial anguish and violent rage, was completely surprising to me: she decided, despite all she had learned, that she would quit her job and come to New York to live with me. No matter how frightened I was, I felt then, in a way that now, in light of all that followed, seems more sadistic than caring, that I owed her *that* much. Yes indeed. I owed her the chance for a life with the man who had hurt her more than anyone else in her adult life had. My generosity was overwhelming. I guess that any relatively healthy relationship that finally got to this point would have been quickly dissolved, but Mandy and I were involved in something that, however painful and terminally unhealthy it may have been, neither of us had the strength to end. It was, or seems to have been, the drama and the trauma to which we were both so helplessly drawn. And so there was more to come.

In the time after my disclosure to her and before her arrival in New York, I watched as Mandy tried, often successfully, to fight the growing urge to attack or kill me. She was generally, though not always, able to restrain herself from physical violence, but seemed completely uninterested in inhibiting the ceaseless and equally violent verbal assaults. And though I undoubtedly deserved much of what I received, it was not a constructive enterprise. If I was as horrible as she was determined to convince me I was, I wondered, why didn't she simply leave me? I know the explanations; I just don't understand them.

There are some things you simply do not, under *any* circumstances, talk about. Here's one.

After telling Leslie about my disclosure to Mandy, and about Mandy's heartbreaking reaction to it, we knew that we could not continue seeing each other. And for a couple of weeks we didn't. Now, what was unacceptable before, was not only unacceptable, it was evil, and we were both smart enough to sense the inevitable conclusion that would be forced upon us by Mandy's impending arrival in New York. Still, without the excuse of ignorance to soothe us and with the knowledge of all that had happened, of all that might yet happen, we allowed our shared lust to have its way with us one or two more unforgivable, guilt-ridden times.

Perhaps part of what enabled me to persist in my activities even after seeing the terrible damage Mandy had sustained was the belief that she was right. I was a horrible human being, so why not act like one? Again, I have no desire to excuse my actions. I would simply like to understand them. I am probably as confused as anyone is. But to say that I tried as hard as I could, would be as dishonest as saying that I never tried at all. I was, much of the time, fighting a fierce internal struggle, moving the battle lines ever so slightly, first one way, and then the other, never actually gaining much ground in either direction. I couldn't, or wouldn't alter my most ingrained behavior, but neither could I seem to give in to it and accept its inevitable consequences.

I have never understood, and I still do not understand the value of a cake you cannot eat, or the point of having permission to eat a cake you do not have. What I *have* finally learned is that you can't have everything you want, and that that is not such a terrible thing. Share the fucking cake. Don't be a pig.

40

My Lucky Break

So Mandy and I rented a U-Haul truck the size of Spain, loaded it with all of her belongings and the remains of my own, and drove to Manhattan, where we sweated and strained as we moved ourselves, unaided, in to the Upper West Side apartment that we'd arranged to sublet from David and Leslie, who had suddenly decided to move out and try their luck at a cowfamily's life in Idaho (maybe David had sensed something). Yes, I was uncomfortably back at the scene of the crime (or one of them), and Mandy was unemployed and living in a dark, dingy apartment in a cold, uncaring city with a man she barely recognized, and with whom she wasn't at all certain she could ever feel safe again. I was aware that with our new living arrangement it would be very difficult to ever again indulge my baser desires, and although at times that seemed like a effective, if forced, control, at other times it felt like the slow, painful, unimaginable death of all hope, of all reason for living.

While Mandy stayed at home, wrapped in a thickening cloak of anger and depression, I worked five days a week at the clothing store, Reminiscence, and continued playing and rehearsing with George and the band in Pennsylvania. Unfortunately, it no longer made much sense to drive out to the Poconos and play with my friends in *Area Code 717*, who sadly disbanded upon receiving my reluctant final resignation.

When I grudgingly accepted the job at Reminiscence—a job for which I had applied fully expecting and hoping that they would recognize my unsuitability for such a position and quickly reject me—I guess I was tacitly acknowledging the cruel reality that I might not *yet* be able to make a living as a musician in New York City. I could have joined a full-time club date band (a band that plays between three and six weddings and bar mitzvahs every weekend for the rest of their sour lives), but I hadn't come to New York to work in the Long Island sparkling-turd wedding mills with yet another bullshit band. I could have done that anywhere. I agreed to take the retail position, with the understanding that I didn't plan to make a career of the clothing business, and that I might, with any luck, require a somewhat flexible schedule. Even after all of that the sadistic bastards hired me.

And I think that, in spite of my absolute indifference and relative ignorance, I did a fairly good job as a clothing salesguypersonman. As has often been the case, I didn't quite feel that I belonged, but the staff and customers generally responded well to me, and I did my best to survive the long days without sustaining or causing too much damage. What I was gradually beginning to discover, so relatively late in my life, and with mixed emotions, was that under most normal circumstances I was fairly effective in my dealings with other humans. They liked me, and to my eternal surprise, I liked a select few of them.

Judy, the store's general manager, was a tall, good-looking, and very pleasant, if solemn, woman. She seemed to like and trust me, and I liked and trusted in return. Nicki Silver, a flamboyant homosexual with a wonderful sense of humor and a vicious cutting wit (he is now a somewhat successful playwright) was, when I embarked upon my new career, a department manager and my immediate superior at the store. In spite of our substantial differences, we became friends. There were those in the organization who were not fond of Nicki, but I appreciated his intelligence and his sense of humor, and we got along exceedingly well. There were other nice and not so nice people on the store's staff, but these two were the heart of the organization and the people with whom I most often voluntarily communicated.

And there were the inevitable hip New York customers who came strutting through the store in desperate search of vintage overcoats (I believe the overcoats came from Germany and I've always wondered, though I never asked, what their ugly histories were), poorly made linen skirts and pants, "cruisewear," and an odd and often unsightly assortment of old and new "antique" clothing and jewelry. There were models and shoplifters and actors and glue-sniffers and singers and winos and ex-cons and exactly the bizarre assortment of characters you might expect to find in a downtown clothing store in Manhattan. Given the dubious quality of the goods we sold, I never understood the store's popularity, but I suppose that in a city of that size, so thickly populated and with such diversity, you can probably find an eager audience for almost anything, at least for a while. That might also explain much of the truly dreadful music and art that has had its successful beginning in New York.

Then, after all the talking and waiting and hoping and doubting, IT finally happened, the event that would change my life and give my career the jolt it needed. George was offered a record deal with a small Japanese record company that had for a couple of years been offering modest recording contracts to some of the lesser known jazz and studio musicians in the States, and selling the albums, tapes, and CDs internationally. We weren't likely to make a lot of money (of course I would have done it for free if they'd asked), but we would be paid union scale for our studio time, and if the album sold there would be residuals. And we would finally have an album, with our names on it…in Japanese.

The problem with hopes and expectations is the inevitable disappointment.

While most albums take months to record, we had only from midnight until five in the morning to record an hour of music with a band comprised of a rhythm section that at this point seldom worked together, and several guest artists, including three percussionists and several studio players who had never before seen or heard the music we were about to obliterate. And George did not choose the finest of our repertoire. I suppose he, or someone in charge of the unsophisticated

operation, felt it was important to record some of his original compositions, which were always the weakest of the material we played. In fact,
his compositional skills left most everything to be desired. *What* melody? So what could and *should* have been an exciting, creative experience, quickly deteriorated into another frustrating example of what was
so very wrong with my life and career, and for that matter, much of the
music business in general.

The engineer had his own unoriginal ideas about how drums should
be tuned and recorded, some idiot added to the mess by suggesting
that we trigger electronic drum sounds with the real drums, and there
were those three percussionists. Nobody had the sense or interest to
stop and listen to how fucking terribly confused and frenetic it all
sounded. The result of these five sweaty hours of sixteenth-note tor-
ment was an album that sold about as well as it should have, and album
to which I've never been able to listen without wincing and twitching
and blushing brightly. It is unforgivably bad.

I don't know if it is just the nature of such things or something specific to my experience; I only know that nothing I allowed myself to
hope for, outside of some of my more stimulating sexual conquests,
was *ever* really satisfying. And I don't think my expectations were
unreasonably high. I guess I just believe that in addition to whatever I
did to attract disappointment, those were the cards I was dealt. Whatever the explanation, if there is one, I was not pleased. Whenever I
allowed myself to want something other than a woman, I was met with
frustration and bitter dissatisfaction. Maybe that is how it generally
works. Perhaps most everyone goes through the same ugly cycle, but
even that doesn't make me feel a hell of a lot better. It is a horrible,
depressing way to trudge blindly through the only life we have. Why
not bury yourself in something that you understand, something you
can control, at least up to the point when you no longer want to control it? Don't we deserve satisfaction of some kind if we're to suffer
through this meaningless muddle; don't we need it? How else can we
sustain an image of ourselves with which we can stand to share a life?

Anyway, those would have been some of my self-serving, self-directed arguments if I'd thought of them at the time. And I probably would have found them just about as compelling as you likely do. But that wouldn't have stopped me.

In spite of all that was wrong with the situation, I continued to play with *Low Profile* (when there was work). Inexplicably, I continued to hope that something good might come of all this pain, that maybe *I* was the one who was mistaken, that the album or the band or I was better than I believed. I even hoped, once or twice, that the few people who might accidentally hear the recording would believe that it was *they* who were wrong, that, in spite of the clear, blaring, undeniable evidence to the contrary, we were a good band playing good music, damn it, and that I, particularly (I *was* Keith Jarrett's brother after all), was a talented musician. Good God. How desperation blinds us.

41

Let Me See if We Have That in Your Size, Babe

It is difficult enough under the best of circumstances to possess or force the discipline necessary to practice with any regularity, so when there are real obstacles it becomes amazingly easy to find a credible excuse to avoid the effort entirely. Living in an apartment in Manhattan, one is immediately offered many compelling excuses.

There is, particularly in the case of a drummer, the limited space, the neighbor on the right, the neighbor on the left, the neighbor above, and the neighbor below. Add to that the distraction of a day job, a city full of beautiful, hypothetically available women frolicking half-naked or more through the steaming streets, or completely naked in the apartment across from and below your own (thank you, whoever you were), and a relationship with a woman who seems to hate you at least as much as she says she loves you, and you will find that you're not getting a hell of a lot of work done. At least that's what *I* found. I spent about a thousand dollars on an electronic drum set to help deal with the problem of the neighbors, but the woman living below was not satisfied, and I had to tiptoe around her in-home work and sleep schedule to avoid an ugly confrontation and likely expulsion from the building, where, though we were paying our rent, we were never formally accepted by the all-knowing, all-powerful nazi coop board. I guess I probably did the best I could, given the confusion and the combination of imagined and very real impediments. Anyway, I did what I did.

Meanwhile, back at the clothing store, I flirted less effectively than in the more comfortable, more familiar environment of a club or concert hall, where I would be a relatively young musician, rather than an aging retail servant. And a great many lovely women passed through the store in search of their dream garments, but though I made an effort, I generally found myself inhibited by the sense that I was less impressive peddling dirndls than playing drums. In addition to all of that, I was now living with Mandy, making it quite a bit more complex than it had ever been before, and a little more difficult to ignore the potential consequences should I find a victim.

At home the atmosphere was funereal, and certainly not conducive to romance or affection. Nevertheless, I tried, and I'm certain Mandy tried as well. But in time we both became aware that we were a couple of profoundly troubled kids, each with emotional problems that went far deeper than those with which we were clumsily contending. All of this was taking a toll on both of us. And my mental health, such as it was, was on a rapid downward trajectory.

Mandy had difficulty finding a position in her ill-chosen profession that either appealed to her or paid enough to compensate her for the intrinsic ugliness of the work. So for a temporary diversion from both the inner and outer turmoil and a little income of her own, she took a part-time job as a cocktail waitress. It may have been a reasonable idea, but it didn't help much. Getting out of the dark apartment was probably a positive thing, but getting in to a dark bar, where she would constantly be approached by men whose licentious behavior only reminded her of mine was not the best choice, though there did not appear to be many options.

At the store I was promoted to the influential position of "department manager" (imagine my excitement), and given an increase in salary as we moved in to a larger location. But the musical work was very sporadic, and I was just barely getting by until I received the fateful phone call from the incredible Claudio Depante' asking me if I'd like to play with his band, *Topaz*. Fuck.

42

"Bark Like a Dog, Geezer"

Jody Ford, Gerry Funkleman's unpleasant wife, had given or sold Claudio my phone number and told him that I might be available to play with them at The King's Arms, a Rockland County nightclub where they were interred on weekends. I did my agonizing paid audition on a Friday night at the club and was immediately punished with a job offer.

Claudio, a fifty year-old Italian immigrant, lived (appropriately) in Bayside, Queens. His weapon of choice was a Hammond organ, tuned to "maximum carnival" setting, with a cheap Radio Shack synthesizer as a potent sidearm. He would have been far more comfortable, I suspect, and more effective with a leaky accordion and a deaf monkey (any self-respecting hearing monkey would have pierced its own eardrums or committed monkeycide). An angry young man named Mike "I hate this fucking gig" Ginex, also from Queens, played guitar acceptably well, and Jody was the perfume-saturated yodeler. Lucky me. My single comment, after noting the inexplicably enthusiastic response of the octogenarian audience that first weekend, was this: "I guess we're set, at least until the audience dies…but what are we going to do *next* week?"

Topaz was a truly terrible band, and I was in a constant state of hyper-shame and embarrassment, living with the fear that someone not both in need of a hearing aid, and excited to still have the energy to leave the "home" for a couple hours before his evening enema, might accidentally happen upon the supper club and witness my complicity in the migraine-inducing cacophony. As far as I now know it never happened, but it might have, and I was haunted by the possibility.

Now let's see. I had come to New York City hoping for the opportunity to develop my musical skills and pursue a career as a jazz and studio drummer. What I found myself doing, more than a year later, was working in a clothing store, playing with an absolutely awful band, and living with a woman who was fighting a losing battle with her growing urge to murder me. This was not my finest hour. Actually, I didn't have a finest hour, did I? Damn.

Occasionally, in response to my increasing frustration, I would look through the "musicians wanted" section of the Village Voice, allowing myself the hope of finding something to inspire my waning interest in music, and in life. I rarely got as far as an audition. The phone call was usually enough to dissuade me from further interest in the, "you know, like scene, dude." And on those rare occasions when I *did* elect to take the next step, it was generally disappointing, if not outright pathetic. Nevertheless, it was through this desperate search, that I ultimately connected with Dan Krimm, who in his ad had stated his intention to record an album that was to be funded by the grant he'd *already* received from the National Endowment for the Arts. Although his ad made it clear that he was looking specifically for a percussionist, and I was, strictly speaking, a drummer, I called him and arranged to go to the studio where they were holding auditions the following evening.

So...

In the small rehearsal studio on the Upper West Side where I met Dan, the scrawny bass player, composer, and proud recipient of the grant, were his friendly and capable pianist, Gary Monheit, and their less impressive flute owner, Jan Notsogood. There were also congas, timbales, and an entire arsenal of percussion paraphernalia ready to be expertly caressed by someone other than me. And sitting off to one side was a drum set. I remember thinking, for an optimistic (see also idiotic) moment, that I might be able to counterfeit the skills required to get through the audition utilizing the various toys they had assembled.

But then I realized that if these musicians were good enough to interest me, they would most likely be good enough to recognize immediately my technical ineptitude, and that even if they didn't, I certainly would.

"Look," I said after my brief internal debate. "I don't want to waste your time *or* my own. I'm really not a percussionist; I'm a drummer. But since we are all here anyway, why don't I just do what I'm most comfortable doing? If nothing else, we'll have the opportunity to play together, and maybe some interesting music will find its way out." Dan smiled and agreed, and without further discussion we played three or four of his compositions.

At the end of the twenty-minute audition we were all, I think, invigorated. It was clear that Dan and his band liked the unexpected transformation his music had undergone at my hands. They were able to see the material in a different light because of the energy and excitement my instrument, and maybe my playing, added. And once again, in spite of my earlier disappointments, I found myself feeling a hint of hope and a sense of possibility. There might yet be a future worth hanging around for.

But...

At The King's Arms Claudio replaced angry Mike with Walter Roberti, a talented young rock guitar player with a terrible voice and a sweet disposition who looked like the Pillsbury Doughboy. Jody, who apparently wanted to make it clear to our victims that *she* was in charge of the horror, suddenly decided that it didn't "look so good" to have the lowly drummer count off the tunes. So I acceded to her authority, generously allowing her to demonstrate her impressive control, smiling sweetly (and sinisterly) behind my drums as we played everything, no matter how ridiculous and awkward, at precisely the tempo she had randomly chosen, playing entire disco songs as dirges and sweet tender ballads as racing polkas. It didn't take long for her to realize the error of her ways. Cretin. And through it all Claudio sat proudly oblivious behind his big wooden weapon, rocking and grinning like the idiot he was as his feet tripped sloppily across the evil bass pedals in search of the wrong note. And the dumb fuck (who at one point had the nerve to defend Adolph Hitler) always found it, after several clunking, dissonant attempts. And the beat, such as it was, went on.

I made friends, in a distant, impersonal way, with John, the aspiring policeman who was and probably still is tending bar at The King's Arms, and with a few of the still breathing customers who thought that I was a gifted and very funny guy, in spite of my radical ideas. I had suggested, for instance, that racism was a bad thing and that poverty was not necessarily a crime, and I expressed the foolish idea that it was inappropriate, and maybe even a bit extreme, to murder the sometimes-annoying but generally harmless men and women who stood on busy street corners washing car windows for tips. I'm sure many of them liked and even respected me, but it was clear that from *their* frighteningly common perspective, I was a little loony.

And I have to admit that when the numerous between-set debates became heated, as they often did, I took pleasure in the impossible challenge of getting my point across to these fossilized minds, or the sick spectacle of watching them squirm. And those who were not stupid, the ones who had simply never heard this unfathomable new perspective, would sometimes budge just a little, clearly uncomfortable with the idea that that which they had always accepted and mindlessly embraced as the truth might possibly be somehow flawed. It was, for me, an interesting cultural education. What I think I learned there was that basically decent people sometimes believe horrible, deadly lies. And I was reminded over and over of what I'd always believed, and continue to believe: that some people, many people, I'm afraid, are simply hideous and contemptible.

The other gruesomely hilarious thing I learned while playing at The King's Arms was that Jody was having some bizarre form of sex with the old decrepit guy, Joe, who often drove her to the club and followed her around carrying her equipment and soaking up the sinus-burning residue of her awful perfume. He was an ugly worm of a man, and it frightens me to think of what might have been going on between them.

"Bark like a dog, geezer."

"Yes, my princess."

"Biscuit?"

Yuck.

The daily routine droned on at the clothing store, and Mandy finally found a job as a counselor in the employee assistance department at Metro North Railroad, giving her the much-needed opportunity to get outside of herself and her own angry drone. The *Dan Krimm Band* rehearsed regularly, and played in a few of the lesser jazz clubs in the city—places where the audience was comprised almost exclusively of friends and relatives who were generous enough to pay to support our habit—in preparation for the album we would soon be recording. I substituted twice for the drummer who was doing the Broadway revival of *The King and I* with Yul Brynner (as he was preparing to croak), and oh, what a bored and boring bunch of blue-collar musicians these Broadway regulars seemed to me. I had a brief and unexciting affair with a cute but tiresome little ballet dancer I'd met at the store who wanted more than just to fuck and suck (what was her problem?), and finally, it was time to record the album. I had my second chance. And though I was suitably skeptical, I allowed for the possibility that this would not be the total devastating disaster that the George Younger album had been.

In spite of a lifetime of experience, and all the tangible evidence of the futility of hope, I had an inexplicable sense of possibility. What is it that drives this idiotic, mindless instinct? How can a relatively intelligent man with an unfailing history of disappointment and dissatisfaction, a man with absolutely no reason to expect anything but the worst, allow himself to be tempted and taken in by the irrational fantasy of sudden unprecedented good fortune? Maybe it is the hope that keeps us going; perhaps without it we would simply shrivel up and die, rather than suffering through redundant cycles of bitter discontent and gradual recovery. Maybe its only purpose is to keep us alive, to keep us writhing in agony just a little longer so that we can live long enough to get our hopelessly hopeful progeny safely into their child bearing years so that they too can suffer long enough to…

Though the product wasn't everything I'd irrationally allowed myself to hope it would be, the process of recording *Sentience*, the Dan Krimm album, was unexpectedly enjoyable and stimulating. Dan fortunately realized before it was too late that Jan was not good enough to be on the album. He hired a gifted saxophonist named Marty Fogel, and a wonderful guitar player, who was a friend of mine, named Vic Juris. I was able to use and tune my own drums, and, at least initially, to have a say in how they were recorded. And Dan and the band had enough respect for me to generally trust my musical instincts, which were sometimes quite good.

This was, compared with George Younger's album, a calm, leisurely process. We had five or six relaxed sessions during which to record the basic tracks for ten songs, with some additional time allotted for dubbing and mixing. We were able to listen to what we had recorded, to learn from it, and do it again if we weren't all satisfied. What a clever concept it was to give the musicians time to get comfortable and establish an environment that was conducive to creativity. The only problem with that was that we were later deprived of one excellent excuse for the album's undeniable mediocrity. Nevertheless, we, or I, at least, found plenty of others. It was really not a completely terrible album. It had its moments, but it was also seriously flawed.

One completely useless thing I learned through this experience was how much damage a recording engineer can do. I knew he (I've intentionally forgotten his name) was stoned most or all of the time, but the more time he spent working on the music, the worse it sounded. My cymbals and hi-hat disappeared completely from one of the better songs, and the natural open drum sound of which I'd been so proud was muffled beyond recognition. An insidious pattern was forming—or simply becoming more apparent to me.

Maybe the more useful part of what I was gradually beginning to understand, was that the purpose of life, if, in fact, there is any purpose at all, is to find a way of accepting and embracing who and what we are, rather than struggling violently against it in the vain search for someone else's elusive image of success and happiness. This is not to say we shouldn't strive to be more; it is simply to suggest that there may be something of value in what we already are, and that many of the goals we choose, or which are chosen for us, may not offer the promise we foresee.

And in spite of her substantial and unrelenting anger, Mandy was, through much of my frustration, incredibly supportive. She sincerely wanted me to be happy and successful in my work, and she did her best, I think, to give me whatever I seemed to need. I guess she believed in me, though I really can't imagine why. And when Mandy was hurt, depressed, or confused about work or family or life in general, or anything other than me, I was there for her, ready, eager to give her anything—well, almost anything she needed. There was no falseness, no selfishness in our concern for one another; it was the purest part of what little remained. It simply wasn't enough to undo the terrible damage we (I?) had done. We would have been better off without it. Without it, maybe we could have escaped earlier, and without so much anguish. It was, at least in part, our tremendous intrinsic empathy for one another that kept us from severing the fraying thread that had bound us uncomfortably together for so long. Yada yada.

Sentience was not a hit. I don't really know how many copies were sold, or if any of them were sold to anyone outside of the same small circle of friends and family that would faithfully appear at the clubs where we played. There was no marketing money and consequently no marketing, and if there was any positive word-of-mouth at all it couldn't have been more than a subdued whisper. In the aftermath of the non-response to the album we continued to play around Manhattan, but it didn't take very long to lose whatever enthusiasm we'd generated amongst ourselves, and it didn't take much longer for us to allow the band to slowly, quietly dissolve. Pfft.

It was at our last live engagement that a familiar looking man who had been sitting at the bar listening intently to the band approached me and introduced himself. He was the drummer from the band I'd played and gotten drunk with at Cave' 54 in Heidelberg years earlier. He had seen my name in the small advertisement the club had placed in the Village Voice, and wanted to hear me play again and say hello. I invited him to sit-in with the band, but, with a friendly smile, he declined. It was nice to see him that night, though I was, for some reason, a little ashamed of my playing. I haven't seen or heard from him or any of the other musicians in his band since, which is probably too bad.

And then...

An odd variety of short-lived bands grew out of the Dan Krimm experience. Dan's friend, Robert Morseberger was assembling an original rock band called *Robert Secret*, which seemed like it might be an interesting change, and at the same time, Marty Fogel, the talented guest sax player from the Dan Krimm album was putting together a jazz quartet. I rehearsed with both groups, the rock band in a dirty basement under a bodega on the Lower East Side block where the Hell's Angels had their headquarters (possibly the safest block in Manhattan), and with Marty's band in his small home in Montclair, New Jersey. Both experiences were sometimes stimulating, and on rare occasion almost inspiring. *Robert Secret* recorded enough material for an album, though not a very good one, and played at a couple of New York's   play-for-free-for-a-few-of-your-friends-and-three-annoying-drunks-in-the-vain-hope-that-there-is-an-important-agent-in-the-room-what-a-pile-of-shit-that-is rock dives before I became frustrated enough to resign, and Marty Fogel's band played out four or five times at colleges and nightclubs and made a no-budget effort at a recording which, in the end, came to nothing, before finally disbanding.

Then, the guitar player from "Robert Secret," Chris Joannou, decided he wanted to record an album of his own compositions, pale imitations, I thought, of Pat Metheny's songs. Why not? Chris was a pleasant lad, and he was not without ability, but his music simply did not hold together. He didn't understand the importance of melody and form, and his writing and playing both lacked confidence and coherence. Blah blah blah...

I tried to learn from all of these disparate experiences, to take something of value from them, even if it was merely the sense of novelty, or the chance to escape from my own thoughts. And though I'm certain each of them offered me a new challenge, an opportunity to learn more about music and about my instrument and maybe myself, the result of all this energy and effort, in terms of my playing and my career, was merely subtle movement to one side or the other, rather than the forward motion I so desired. Therefore, when I received the call from April Newman, an old friend and reasonably talented singer who was employed with her boyfriend David Scott at Tamiment, yet another glamorous Pocono resort, I reluctantly and conditionally accepted their offer of steady work. They would pay me fairly well, enabling me to quit both the clothing store and the haunting nightmare with *Topaz*, and they were willing, initially at least, to allow me the freedom to take any other more interesting work (such as dusting) I might get, as long as I sent in a suitable (as in breathing) substitute to suffer in my place.

43

Eat Your Greens, Fucker

Of course I recognized the distressing significance of my decision. I knew that taking the job at Wayne Newton's Understandably Bankrupt Tamiment Resort might be the first tentative step backwards. I knew, or assume I must have known, that my willingness to do this suggested the beginning of a sad submission to dreadful reality. But though I was not pleased, I simply didn't see a preferable alternative.

And, of course, Mandy was not pleased at all. She'd left an entire life behind in Pennsylvania to come to New York and live with me while I pursued a musical career, and now I was working in the Poconos again, four, sometimes five nights a week. I think she understood how depressing it had been working at the clothing store and playing with "*Topaz*", but it would have been impossible to fool either of us into believing this was a step forward.

I'd had a crush on April when I was sixteen, and for several years after, and though I'm reasonably certain she shared my youthful romantic interest, neither of us had ever acted upon it with more than a tentative kiss. By the time we met again at Tamiment, April had been married to an quiet little man with a thick beard, given birth to two children without beards, and suffered for years under the imposition of a strict macrobiotic diet before taking the children, leaving the man and his beard, and eating a couple dozen buttery Lumberjack breakfasts at Denny's. Now she was singing at Tamiment, raising her healthier kids, and living with David, who, though he had no beard and was not surviving on twigs and ferns, was many other kinds of weird.

David was not a terrible keyboard player, but to keep the band's expenses to a minimum (more money in his own bottomless pockets), he played left hand bass, leaving me once again without a real bass player and only half a keyboard player. And though I did come to like David, I learned very quickly that it would be completely insane to ever trust him when it came to anything involving money. David *always* lied, even when there was no reason, or when he realized that there was about a ninety-eight percent chance that he would eventually be caught. In short, he could not help it, and therefore was, in a sense, innocent. He meant no harm. He was also driven by ritualistic behavior. He walked carefully along the same route from their trailer on the grounds of the resort to the lounge where we played every night so that he could be certain to greet the trees that might otherwise be upset at his absence. I think David sincerely liked me too, but he probably would have given me up to the authorities for a crime I hadn't committed for a ten-dollar bounty. The fact is that for ten dollars he might have confessed himself if there was no one else around to accuse.

Another of David's more notable peculiar behaviors was his dinner ritual. He could not leave one shriveled pea, one soggy kernel of corn, or a single mealy speck of overcooked potato skin on his plate without feeling an unbearable sense of guilt; he was certain that the poor morsels left behind would feel abandoned. The great thing about this particular expression of his mental illness was that on those occasions when I was angry at him because I'd just learned, for instance, that the band had received a massive raise two months earlier because the management liked the new singer-drummer so much and David had been greedily pocketing the money, I could order lots of extra vegetables for myself and simply keep piling them onto his plate, a few at a time, saying in a sad, sad vegetable voice, "Please don't leave me, please" as he bloated up to unrecognizable proportions. And I did.

I'd like to believe that my efforts on behalf of David's gradually increasing acreage played a small part in the wonderful event that occurred one afternoon several months after I'd been hired and cheated out of thousands of dollars that were rightfully mine to squander.

Apparently, many trailers don't have bathtubs, but David's did; as a registered obsessive compulsive he was unwilling to live without this luxury. In fact, he insisted upon taking long leisurely baths every afternoon prior to his routine pre-dinner nap. As local legend has it, David was lying back in the full tub on that particular brisk winter Sunday afternoon when he felt something rumble and shift beneath him. "April," he called out calmly, "did you feel…" and the entire tub went crashing through the trailer floor, spilling out onto the cold, hard ground, where David lay, stunned and naked for all the world to see. Steam poured from his hairy body as he gazed around him in confused horror, curious neighbors opening their windows and doors to investigate the source of the clamor. Really.

Working with David and April was good clean fun, and they enjoyed my sense of humor, but there was very little music involved in the enterprise, and the remains of my mind and heart were elsewhere, if anywhere at all. And for some reason, though God knows I tried, I just couldn't seem to get laid at Tamiment. My time with the trio finally came to a welcome end when I was offered more money to play with a better band at a resort that was about ten miles closer to home.

44

The Butts

T he perfect, sad symbolism was certainly not lost on Mandy or me when Tee, who had by this time been sober for a couple years, and was working again, called me and asked me to come back to Fernwood and play with the new band he had assembled—to replace, as it turned out, the out-of-control alcoholic drummer with whom they'd been suffering. Tee even acceded to my stipulation that I be allowed to take other work if I wanted to (enabling me to at least keep the fantasy of a future alive a little longer). And he agreed to make certain there would be a room for me at the hotel at least one night a week so that I could occasionally avoid the long boring commute back to New York (and for other reasons I didn't bother to disclose). I was, once again, back at Fernwood, with the new and somewhat improved *Tee and Company*. An ugly circle (or was it a spiral?) completed.

The new band was actually quite good, and even fun for a while. For the first month of my return visit to Fernwood, Jimmy Tigue was the nervous, gray-haired, and indescribably peculiar organ player, but Jimmy soon decided to move on and was immediately replaced by a massive bearded keyboard player named Lou Czsckskjptcvklk, whose parents had come from a small Eastern European country that was so impoverished that they couldn't afford vowels. Lou was a competent player and a well-meaning person. Mercifully, he didn't even own an organ. But he would ramble endlessly about topics he didn't seem to fully understand, and about which I didn't care at all, and always, as he blathered, I would hear my own desperate voice crying out in my mind, "Shut up, *please* shut the fuck up."

There was the prerequisite female singer, a slightly-plump, mildly-competent, lily-white, pinched-nosed, priggish piddle named Tracy Golly-Gee, who despite all of that was probably a nice enough human being and not a completely awful singer, but whom I found terribly annoying nonetheless. And finally, there was Nancy Reed, large, Black, sweet, smart, gifted, and smiling brightly. Nancy, who is married to a gifted guitar player-singer by the name of Spencer Reed, was and is a wonderful singer and a good guitar player. She had learned to play bass specifically for the job at Fernwood, and she was, for me, the best thing about that band. Tee was an excellent musician of course, and a dear friend, but Nancy is one of the sweetest, funniest people I've ever known, and she was becoming a very competent bass player. If I could have a sister, it would be Nancy, and I think she might feel the same way, so maybe I have a sister, whereas Tee is far too tall to be my brother.

Tee and Company worked five short, easy nights a week for what was, at the time, decent money, while life with Mandy, instead of stabilizing as I'd vainly and probably stupidly hoped, was becoming more strained. Her anger was making its way to the turbulent surface virtually every day now, and we were both frustrated and deeply depressed. When we communicated at all it was to do battle or to share only the worst of what we were thinking and feeling. There was little joy or tenderness, and less laughter. And passion, except for that which was expressed in the form of violence to the furniture or walls, was a fading distant memory. No one was happy.

So...

On the nights when I finished work early I would go out in search of a firm, moist distraction before driving back to New York, where I would spend a frustrating hour or so hunting for the only available parking space on the Upper West Side. And once a week, when I stayed overnight at the hotel, I would try even harder, sometimes actually succeeding in finding a willing victim, while at others, going back to my lonely, often sub-standard room to read or masturbate with impressive fervor. I tried to obscure my knowledge of the state my life was in, in any way, in every way possible.

Every summer the Pocono Mountain resorts fill up with a new group of waiters and waitresses, mostly college kids who wanted to make a little beer money to get them through the hot summer months. Allison Ashford, a pretty, blond seventeen-year-old (with a slender seventeen-year-old body) who stood checking orders and collecting money at the cash register in the hall of doom between the two noise chambers known as The Gaslight Lounge and The Astor Room, was one of the more interesting new recruits that next summer at Fernwood. I began my assault with a few smiles, worked my way up to mild verbal sparring, and finally, I did the obvious thing: I bought her a lollipop. That's right, a lollipop. After that, of course, all that was left was to ask her out, which I did one evening after work.

It took surprisingly little coaxing to get Allison to agree to a late night swim at Smithfield Beach, a tiny patch of dirty sand along the banks of the Delaware River just a few miles south of the resort. It took no coaxing at all to get her to tear off all her clothes and jump, pale and naked, into the fortunate dark water. There was not much swimming that night. And though we didn't sleep together, we got awful dirty setting the stage for a future meeting, when we would be able to finish what we'd begun in a more comfortable setting.

The following Wednesday night, when I asked Allison if she would like to get together again, she smiled a sexier smile than should be possible or legal for one so young, and said, "I bought the wine." We had one quick drink at the bar before making our way up to the honeymoon suite that had been secured for me by my helpful new friend at the front desk.

And so…

Naked in the bubbling whirlpool, Allison shyly confessed that she had come to Fernwood months earlier to visit her older sister, who was working as a waitress there, and that when she saw me on the stage that night, she decided she wanted to sleep with me. I told her, as several quarts of blood drained from my arms, legs and head, making their way to my quickly expanding primary appendage, which was now poking at my throat, that I was always happy, without any regard whatsoever for my own selfish desires, to help people satisfy their fantasies. We leapt from the tub and fucked and sucked for hours on a round bed under a mirrored ceiling. One of us had a great butt.

After that, every Wednesday night, with an occasional Tuesday or Thursday night thrown in as a bonus, was spent in essentially the same magnificent way.

Allison was bright, sexy, very mature, exactly half my age, and completely aware of what was going on between us. During the course of that summer she gave me something wonderful to look forward to every week. And shortly before our time together was about to come to an end Allison made a second shy confession. She said that she loved me, and that, although she knew I didn't love her, and that I was living with someone else, it was a beautiful and welcome feeling—a feeling of which she'd always feared she was incapable. Okay. So, wanna fuck? Actually, I liked her quite a bit too. Really.

Okay. So, wanna fuck?

But this time in my life, like one or two others, was most notable for the disparity between what it probably looked like from the outside and what it felt like from within. From the outside, I must have appeared to be a funny, proficient drummer, working regularly when so many others were struggling to survive, living with a bright, attractive woman in New York, debauching an interesting variety of lovely friends and strangers, and laughing my sad little ass off much of the time. But inside I was bitterly depressed, plagued by guilt or the fear of being caught—plagued still by the haunting image of Mandy's terrible anger and pain, guilty for my inability or unwillingness to find satisfaction with the very special woman who had suffered with so much of my unrestrained, uncaring behavior, the woman who said she *still* loved me in spite of the hatred she regularly, and very effectively expressed. I was bitter about the state of my career and my apparent inability to move on, to improve or to take another chance.

I had spent a painful lifetime constructing the evidence of my most powerful fears, and at that, if at nothing else, I had been an unqualified success. I had no love, no career, and no sense of the good, decent human being who was still theoretically alive, but if so, receding daily into the darkest depths of my silently tortured soul. I was having a wonderful fucking time, and I was spreading the joy to anyone who dared come close.

I guess it has always taken me an inordinately long time to recognize when something is over, or to accept it, or, maybe most importantly, to be willing to deal with it. So maybe it should be no surprise that I allowed myself to suffer through a moribund relationship and a stagnant career at the same time. But life in New York, or what there was of it, had finally become so terrible that I found I wanted nothing more than to escape, even if only temporarily, from the ugliness at home. So when I learned that my old basement apartment in Lore's house in Henryville was available again I rented it immediately. Why not? Why *not* leave Mandy completely while still holding out to her the hope that even I didn't really believe, the hope that I might be coming back after "a couple months" of sorting out my life, happier and healthier, ready to love her as she needed and most certainly deserved? Why *not* go backwards in every way possible to wallow, to bury myself even deeper in my sick, sad, desperate depression? What did I have to lose? And why am I asking you?

I don't remember why Tracy gave notice to the band; I'm just glad she did, and yet that left us with the problem of finding a suitable replacement.

Auditioning singers can be an interesting, even educational experience, I'm sure. Unfortunately, for us the options were limited to a variety of unexceptional young and mostly not-so-young women, many of whom were, at best, only one or two small steps above "talent show" quality. Because of the timeframe imposed upon us, and the mediocre selection, we soon hired a well-constructed and nearly adequate singer, cocaine addict, and sex maniac named Shelly Barge.

"Hey honey, why don't we have dinner some time?" was the mantra Shelly repeated, as night after night, week after week, feeling the warning warming in my tuxedo pants, I wriggled uneasily away. It wasn't really a lack of interest that discouraged me from accepting her blatant requests for my loins. It was simply that I knew she would be there if I really needed her, and that we had to work together, which could easily become awkward if I allowed anything to happen between us. I was also aware that someone as insistent as Shelly was had most likely fucked a lot of guys, and this was shortly after the ugly beginning of the depressing change that would need to take place in human sexual behavior if we were to survive the relatively new and horrific scourge of AIDS.

But she wiggled her cute little butt night after night, and every night it was a new struggle to resist her increasingly aggressive assaults.

March: "Hey honey, why don't we see a movie?"

April: "Hey honey, want to fool around?"

May: "Hey sweetie, why don't we just go fuck our brains out in the Edwardian Room?"

June: "Honey? Can I suck your cock tonight after work?"

July: "I have my vibrator in the car. I'd like to show you how I use it when I'm alone, thinking about having your cock up my ass."

August: "Have I told you about my girlfriend? Sometimes we lick and suck each other's cunts for hours. Why don't you come along sometime and fuck us both?"

"Uh, okay."

I know there are those of you who are thinking as you read this, "I'd give anything for a *good* book." But there are probably also a few of you who are thinking, "This son of a bitch is incapable of exercising any self-restraint at all."

It is to those skeptics that I speak when proudly relating the following story.

In the summer following the one I spent boinking young Allison, another lass was hired to do the same job Allison had done the previous year. It was Allison's younger sister, Andrea. She was every bit as lovely as her older sister, and I assumed she must have heard some reasonably good reviews, so in a selfless effort to stop any ugly sibling rivalry before it even began, and to feel close to Allison in her absence, I brandished my alleged charm on her younger sister immediately. But to my credit, and as proof positive that I am not the horrible monster some of you may think I am, I had the discipline, good taste, and strong moral sense to recognize, after several desperate, pathetic attempts, Andrea's absolute indifference toward me. So there. Judge not, lest ye thine own self get the heebie-jeebies, or something. I bet *that* would have made Mandy proud.

Anyway...

One of the many bands Fernwood hired to entertain and confuse their Saturday night crowds was a self-contained group named *The Sherrels* (I think). Three capable, extra-large, Black women with the largest butts I, or, I dare say, anyone has ever seen, stood in front of an amazed audience singing a medley of their hit and making joke after joke about their own studio apartment size asses, upon which, by the way, the backup band could easily have rested their sheet music, drinks, and drummer. After the show I approached the lead singer and proud proprietor of the largest of these mammoth protuberances. "If you ever decide to change the name of your band," I said. "I have an excellent suggestion."

"Really? What is it?" She put her hands on her mini-van bearing hips and smiled.

"*No ifs or ands.*"

45

The Beginning of the End

I continued to practice, though with steadily decreasing enthusiasm, I continued poking and prodding the local and visiting talent, and I continued, when I dared to consider the question at all, to wonder what the fuck I was doing. To keep Mandy hanging on, to keep myself from feeling too guilty, and to remain in touch with the only woman I had ever known who seemed able to love me in spite of my many failings (the ones she knew about, anyway), a woman that I still, in my own pathetic way, loved, and with whom I desperately wished I could be happy, I drove into New York late every Saturday night and stayed until Monday morning. Of course this wasn't nearly enough to sustain even the sparse remains of our tattered relationship, and so Mandy's confusion and frustration grew. And her completely understandable anger and depression only pushed me farther away. Or maybe that was just another of my many excuses.

But what was so amazing, and sometimes frustrating to me, was Mandy's stubborn refusal to give up. She hung on tenaciously to the bleak emptiness and bitter resentment that was all we had left, only occasionally half-heartedly threatening surrender to our dissolution. And though I wanted her to finally end this misery—*I* certainly wasn't going to do it—I didn't want to hurt her and I didn't want to lose her. I wanted to leave her, but the thought of life without her was terrifyingly, unbearably sad. We were both, I'm afraid, lost in the familiar hollow corpse of a long, destructive lie.

So I spent my days obsessively cleaning my small lonely apartment, practicing, reading, playing chess with my old friend Mark (with whom I'd recently become reacquainted), and, when I stopped the flurry of meaningless motion for more than a minute, trembling with wrenching sadness and fear about who and what I'd become or seemed to be quickly becoming. My nights were spent on the same stage I'd been on so many nights before, singing, playing, and laughing *with* Nancy and *at* everyone else in my path. And we laughed long and hard, sometimes so hard that when it was time for one of us to sing, there was no chance in hell of getting a single word out without gagging or losing a mouthful of saliva. And Tee would stand there, frustrated and angry at first, and then, on his better nights, he too would get caught up in the stupid uncontrolled hilarity, so that we might play entire songs wheezing and turning crimson without ever actually singing an intended note or an intelligible word.

We laughed at the dancers and at the drunks and at the comedians and mostly at each other. We changed the words to suit our moods "So re-grease me and let me love again" and altered the rhythms to stay awake. We played well some nights and slept through others, and on the breaks Nancy and I sat together in the stinking lobby or at the dingy bar and laughed some more or talked about life and how we really felt and acted the way dear friends should and then laughed some more while Lou and Tee sat motionless at the bar, broad, lumpy bodies in worn tuxedoes dispassionately debating sports and politics or staring straight ahead, bored to death, but preferring that mindless tedium, for some reason, to playing another set of stale music.

We played the video games until they refused our quarters, we fatigued the poor staff with our music, and about once every six months we learned a new song that we would come to hate before we ever played it again. Much of the time we could have been stuffing envelopes.

And then something happened. Fernwood had, for some inexplicable reason, become dissatisfied with our band. They were threatening, if we didn't start doing whatever it was that they thought (or knew) we weren't already doing, to replace us with a younger, hipper, and probably less expensive band. It might have made perfect sense, but it scared the poop out of us all.

First, they suggested that we replace Nancy, then it was Lou; even Tee's job was not secure. I suppose I was still young enough, thin enough, white enough to fit their image of what the audience might find appealing, so, for a time I was probably safer than anyone. My greatest fear was that I would either have to survive there without Nancy, or the entire band would be fired and I would die.

What was so frightening to me about what was happening was that I knew that I had no other marketable skills, that without this job I would have nothing, no job, no money, no identity, and no convenient pool of innocents to corrupt in my insatiable venery. But there were other resorts and other bands and I was certainly good enough to play with any of them, so there was more to my terror than even *I* realized at the time. What I now believe was scaring the shit out of me was the slowly dawning awareness (duh) that although this was all I knew how to do, I didn't want to do it any more. I just didn't want to do it any more. There was no denying that I was a much better drummer than I'd been years before; there was no doubt that I could do just what I was doing for the rest of my desolate, unfulfilling, pointless life. My God. Or whomever. The fact was that the only thing more terrifying to me than losing my job was keeping it. Nevertheless, we hung on for a while, promising to learn new music and modernize and lose weight and smile more and kiss their stupid fucking asses in any way the fucking assholes wanted. And for a while they waited, but the fact is that we never did a goddamned thing. We were more tired and disgusted than anyone else was, than anyone else could have been. And in the spring of 1990 we were finally fired. Thank God. Or whomever.

46

Enough Already

Despite my growing awareness that music was not going to offer me what it had tentatively promised—or maybe it was that I had nothing to give to it—I didn't feel I had much choice but to continue searching for work as a drummer. It was still the only thing I knew. Tee looked for and found intermittent work for the band at private parties, weddings, and even for a short while at another nearby resort. I also did some freelance work with a variety of local bands whenever one or another of the other drummers wanted or needed a night off. But even with all of that I was still barely making a living, so when Fernwood refused, arguing that we had not "really" been employees, to pay the unemployment benefits to which we felt certain we were entitled, Lou, Nancy, and I (despite Tee's adamant unwillingness to cooperate and his laughable admonition that if we insisted on following through, we would never have the pleasure of working there again) filed a suit against the resort with the friendly and surprisingly helpful folks at the department of unemployment.

For about a year, while unwaveringly declining any threat of more regular employment, I played in various resorts and clubs and recording studios with anyone who was either willing to pay me, or could inspire the remnants of my waning interest. I played and recorded with George and his band du jour, I played with Nancy and Spencer at the Delaware Water Gap Jazz Festival, and, as always, I did my best to corrupt the morals of myriad members of the female population whenever possible. But in all of this activity there was not even the vaguest sense of direction. It was simply a way to keep busy enough to avoid dealing with the unpleasant reality of my dire life circumstances.

About a year after Fernwood had rid themselves of us I was offered a job in a rhythm and blues band called *The Steamin' Jimmies*. For some reason I can't even begin to recall, I accepted it. They were a group of middling local musicians who had developed an enthusiastic following and were able to work fairly steadily on Friday and Saturday nights at many of the noisy, smoky bars and nightclubs scattered randomly throughout Northeastern Pennsylvania and New Jersey, with a rare excursion into New York City. It was fun playing with these guys—for about ten minutes.

My idea of my role as the drummer in this band, and my notions about creativity in general (now that I had notions) were at odds with those of the powers that were, and particularly those of Phyllis, who was the second and last singing female bass player with whom I worked. And she may have been right, if there is such a position in these debates, but that never stopped me from fighting. And to be fair, although she was not a great bass player, she was certainly not the only musician I'd ever played with who thought my playing should be less busy and complex, more restrained. I suppose I probably learned something through this experience, but I probably didn't care a hell of a lot any more. I was just making a feeble living and getting laid, again, as I had done twenty years before, when I was seventeen and it was probably, by some bizarre standards, okay.

And so…

I bought a racing bike and made friends with Bill Vitulli, the owner of the bike shop, a sweet guy who soon asked me to help him out a couple days a week, which I did partly because I liked him, partly because it was a change, and partly to test the waters again of something outside of the music business. Mandy and I fought and argued. She actually hit me in the face once, to which I responded, "That's the second last time you will do that," before punctuating my strange half-threat by drinking half a bottle of Jack Daniel's. And I watched, apparently helpless, as my life continued its mad, eager dash toward chaos.

I rode my bike for pleasure and exercise, spent time with Mandy out of guilt and sad desperation, played music out of habit, the fear of change, and the need to survive, fucked and sucked out of habit, obsession, a desperate ego, and haunting loneliness, practiced to fool myself into believing there was a reason to practice and to fill the time, began keeping a journal of my agony to document my inevitable fall, worked with George to remind myself of all that was so very wrong with my chosen profession and to keep deadly hope barely alive, drank too much, drove too fast, lied to everyone including myself, sat on the roof tempting cancer and swatting big black flies by the dozen, won the suit against Fernwood, collecting a lump sum of almost five thousand dollars, read to give myself hope and company, cried alone to remember that I cared so very much and because I simply couldn't help it, quit, or was fired from *The Steamin' Jimmies*, moved back to New York to live again with Mandy, took a job playing with my dear friend Nancy and a trio she'd assembled to work weekends in the new Black resort that had recently opened in the Poconos, bought a new car when my truck died, totaled my new car on a rainy highway in Harrisburg, where Mandy, for some reason or no reason at all, thought she might want us to move (as if there was any chance we would ever move anywhere together), and felt myself finally beginning to realize that there was really nothing left. Nothing at all. Not a thing. Not a fucking thing.

It simply wasn't going to be enough for me any longer to be what I was: an adequate drummer spending his life playing for fucking drunks and backing up fucking amateurs and playing the funny fucking hat contest in a fucking place where "amandine" always, without fail, followed "string beans." What the fuck is that about? And why is there no "L" in "amandine?" I had reached my personal best, which, for me, was not good enough. I was not giving anything to anything or anyone; I was not getting anything in return. There was no reason to continue—I was no longer a kid, the money was not enough, the music was always disappointing, and there was no reason in the world to continue doing this thing that paid so poorly, gave me little or no pleasure, and was often deeply frustrating.

If given the choice between two unsatisfying occupations, one wherein you care very much about the process and the product, and the other wherein you care very little or not at all, the choice is, or should be, clear. If you don't care, it hurts far less when it sucks, and if my experience is any indication there is a very, very good chance that it *will* suck, often.

So...

In 1990, at the age of thirty-six, I quit playing music. After all, I no longer had a car. How the hell was I suppose to transport my drums?

A year and a half later—eight years ago and several years too late—I finally left Mandy for the last bitterly, unspeakably sad time.

Epilogue

In the end—and for those of you who have been waiting impatiently, this is the end—I never became the drummer I'd ultimately allowed myself to hope I might somehow magically become, the drummer my most faithful and enthusiastic followers already foolishly believed I was. But I was probably not quite as bad either as my worst fears and harshest judgments regularly and ruthlessly pronounced. On the other hand, as a carbon-based life form and a citizen of the planet earth, I was, at times, every bit as horrible as anyone, including both those who loved me and those who hated me (and there was an ample supply of each), ever could have imagined, although I was also, on rare occasion, as good and loving and giving as I could ever wish to be. Hmm.

And upon learning of my wise decision to quit playing music, or whatever it was that I was then playing had become, my brother Keith, who had never said or done a fucking supportive thing in his bleak, lonely life, took the time to call me and say, "This is very disappointing, Grant. I *really* think you have something to offer as a drummer." How the fuck would he know? In the final ten years of my career, the only years that mattered in terms of music, he never heard me play. Not a note. Not a single note. Not one. Shame on you, Keith.

And finally, for those who might wonder what eventually happens to those of us who struggle in bitter futility for so many years trying to make a career and a life out of a small kernel of inherent ability and the inconstant power of a tentative will, the answer is, I have learned my lesson well. I have given up the foolish notion, the distant idiotic dream that it is possible to support one's self, either financially or in terms of the needs of a large but poorly supported ego, in the highly competitive, extremely challenging, and always frustrating creative world. Looking back, I can barely believe I ever thought it possible.

It was for those reasons, and one or two others, that I ultimately made the pragmatic decision to pursue a much less complicated, less demanding, and less maddening career as writer.

I'm no idiot.

"Be not too liberal; it doth belong
To dogs alone to fuck the whole day long."

—Friedrich Nietzsche

About the Author

Grant Jarrett spent the first twenty years of his working life as a professional musician, and the six years following managing a small business in Manhattan and writing his first memoir. In the past six years he has written over a dozen short stories, two novels, and a second memoir. Mr. Jarrett lives in New York City and earns his living as an editor and freelance writer. In 2001 he published half a dozen magazine articles and ghostwrote a nonfiction book for Pocketbooks.

0-595-23798-3